DECORATING

WITH FABRIC

AN
IDEA BOOK

BY

JUDY LINDAHL

Brand names are mentioned in this book only to indicate consumer products which I have personally used and with which I have been pleased. I am not subsidized by anyone and there may very well be other products that are comparable or even better about which I am unaware.

About the Author: Judy Buess Lindahl is a free lance home economist residing in Portland, Oregon. She was graduated from Washington State University with honors and received her B.S. in Home Economics Education. After graduation she taught home economics in Beaverton, Oregon before leaving to join the educational staff at Simplicity Pattern Company of New York. As an educational fashion stylist Judy traveled the country presenting programs in schools and for 4-H, extension, and consumer groups for five and a half years. In 1973 she created a program of ideas and inspiration for decorating with fabrics which she has presented across the United States and Canada. She is the author and publisher of The Shade Book, and author of Decorating with Fabric, a hardback published by Butterick Publishing Co. She has done writing, television, and demonstration work for Fieldcrest sheets. Currently Judy is teaching seminars and classes on a free lance basis. She is married and the mother of two daughters, and has been featured in Outstanding Young Women of America and Personalities of the West and Midwest.

CONTENTS

INTRODUCTION

This book is about a love affair with fabric--because of the way it drapes and shapes, can be stiffened or padded, quilted or stuffed, stapled, fused, glued or starched.

Decorating with Fabric contains a collection of ways fabric can be used in do-it-yourself decorating, and is intended as a resource to use again and again to help you create your own special environment. Let it guide you as you apply fabric to walls, construct and cover folding screens, create window treatments, cover lampshades and turn the ordinary into the exceptional!

Most of all, I hope it inspires you to try new things, gives you the confidence to experiment, and helps remove the "fear of failure" that keeps many of us from doing the projects we have wanted to try. A project may not always turn out exactly as you had pictured it, but it can be near enough to delight you. It is the learning, the doing, and the accumulating experiences that will all add to your confidence factor. Dig in! And happy decorating!

FABRIC WALLS

From earliest times man has covered his walls with fabric. Heavy tapestries once provided insulation as well as beautification in drafty villas and castles. Today fabric walls are enjoying a much deserved revival. Whether you put it up yourself or have it professionally installed, you are sure to enjoy the results.

WHY FABRIC WALLS?

Fabric creates excitement through color. It can conceal or give added texture. It can be as temporary as you need. Put it up, live with it for several years, and if you move-- it can go, too. Of course it might never go back on a wall. It could become curtains, slipcovers, fun furniture, pillows, napkins, place mats, or a tablecloth, too.

Fabric can be 'coaxed' over small obstructions and imperfections. Walls do not have to be perfectly smooth, and seldom have to be sized or specially prepared.

Because of the porosity and texture--fabrics can serve as insulators and accoustical aids. Fabric makes a perfect background for wall groupings. The hangar holes won't show-- even when you change your mind.

Walls are seldom straight, and fabric can be stretched or eased to fit--an added advantage.

Note: Knit fabrics are making their appearance in home decorating, too. Everything from slipcovers to wall coverings, bedspreads to tablecloths are giving decorating a new look and expanded dimension.

How long can you expect fabric to be left on a wall? Literally for years!! Exactly how long will depend on the care and the traffic it gets. Fabric will last for many years in a bedroom where it receives little abuse. You may expect to have to change it more often in a kitchen or bath. I know, however, of several cases where fabric had been on kitchen walls for nearly six years.

One of the most frequently asked questions is, "which is more economical--fabric or wallpaper?" That will depend on each situation, your taste in fabric, your selection of wallpaper. But remember--wallpaper is usually 18" to 28" wide. Fabric is 36", 45", 54"--even 58" or 60". Wallpaper is purchased in a roll, often a double or triple roll. Fabric can be purchased closer to amount needed. And you have the advantage of using the same fabric for walls, curtains, roller shades, etc. Thus the dye lot will always match.

Perhaps the best advantage of all is that in most instances you can retreive the fabric for another use when you choose to remove it and re-decorate.

BEFORE YOU BEGIN

ANALYZE THE ROOM to help you decide just where and how you will use the fabric.
NOTE: Bathrooms are small rooms, but complicated because of all the objects around which fabric must be fitted.

MEASURE WALLS not only for size, but also to determine whether ceiling is straight. Measure at points indicated by arrows.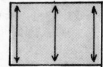

EXAMINE THE SURFACE TEXTURE OF THE WALL. If you wish to place fabric on a wall to conceal texture, this must be considered in the method and fabric you choose.

WHAT IS THE CONSTRUCTION of the wall? Plaster, tile, concrete, sheetrock and paneling can all be covered with fabric; however, construction influences the method of application you will select.

3

WHAT COLOR IS THE WALL? Light colored fabrics may not successfully cover darker tones or prints. If dark or bright colored fabrics are not colorfast, they could fade onto a light colored wall, if the method of fabric application uses moisture.

Consider the Fabric

Here are some guidelines to consider as you search for the perfect fabric for your room--
- Firmly woven fabrics are the easiest to work with.
- All-over prints are the easiest to apply. They keep the observer's eyes moving and best conceal imperfections in application, cracks, texture in wall surface, or an uneven ceiling line.
- Fabrics with an all-over pattern (A) will show soil much less than very open ground patterns (B).

- White and light background prints will be more likely to show some soiling sooner than colored background prints.
- Fabrics with horizontal stripes or obviously horizontal design motifs can call attention to an uneven ceiling.

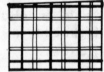 

- Decorator fabrics are printed with a design overlap near the selvages, which create a perfect pattern match when a fabric is seamed.
- Be aware of the distance between the design repeat. Large repeats require additional yardage for matching.

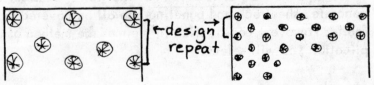

- Note whether the design is a drop match (A) or a straight across match (B). A drop match is a visual trick to make the design appear larger.

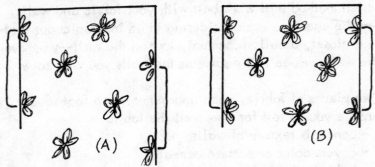

(A)   (B)

- Wide fabrics require fewer seams, but they may need extra hands for easier application.
- If the lengthwise grain is somewhat stretchy, removing the selvages will permit more even stretch and hang of fabric.
- Fabric must be able to withstand moisture if glue, paste, or starch will be used.'
- Fabrics that will be stapled should be as nearly on grain as possible. Since the pattern must be hung straight on the wall--grainline that is too far off can cause drag lines as the fabric relaxes.

Note: It is important to drape several feet of the fabric and then back off to view it from 10 to 15 feet away. Colors and designs that seem important at 6" often disappear from a distance. Try to view the fabric as you would in a room. It is even better to view it in the room where you plan to put it. Thus you can check for lighting effects and color coordination.

Consider the Methods of Application

The methods of application listed below are detailed further in this chapter. Be sure to read this chapter thoroughly before making a final selection.

- Stapling - directly to wall
  - seamed panels
  - using furring strips
- Starching
- Wallpaper Paste - cellulose or vinyl
- Gluing
- Panels
- Shirring'
- Double-Faced Tape

Make a Test Sample

It is always advisable to make a test sample to determine which method will work best with your fabric and walls. Try the ones you are considering in an inconspicuous spot-- in a closet, a hall, basement, low on the wall--wherever the wall surface is the same as the walls you will cover.

Two pieces of fabric, each approximately a foot square, will enable you to test for how well the fabric --
  - conceals texture of walls
  - covers color or pattern beneath
  - holds to the wall
  - resists shrinking or fading
  - conceals staples

Plan to include a seam or two in the test sample so you can check for shrinkage as well as the ease of cutting, butting, overlapping, or backtacking a seam. (see pp. 10-14)

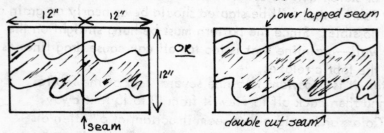

12"   12"   OR   over lapped seam

12"

↑seam   double cut seam↗

Measuring

Determining the amount of fabric you need is not difficult, just follow through step by step. (Bless those calculators!)

Begin by thinking of the number of fabric strips or panels that you will need to cover the area you have chosen.

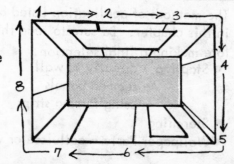

1   2   3

8   4

7   6   5

STEP ONE - DETERMINING THE NUMBER OF PANELS

1. Add the corner to corner measurements of the walls to be covered.

   (A) _____ inches
   (B) _____ inches
   (C) _____ inches
   (D) _____ inches

   (E) _____ Total Inches

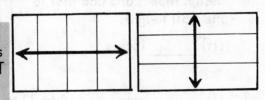

Note: For ceilings or
floors measure across
direction panels will
be applied.

2.

$$\frac{\text{(F) number of panels needed*}}{\text{(E) total inches}}$$

usable width
of fabric in
inches

*Add an extra panel if the
number is uneven. Example:
6 + 24" = 7 panels

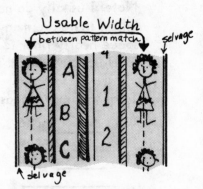

Usable Width
between pattern match
selvage
selvage

Measure actual usable inches of design. This eliminates
selvages and overlap.

STEP TWO - DETERMINING PANEL LENGTH

1. Measure ceiling to baseboard

   (G) _____ inches

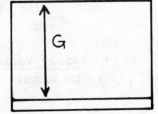

7

For ceiling or floor measure
with the direction panels
will be applied.

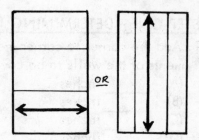

OR

2. Measure the distance between
design repeat and add that to
the wall height.

   (H) _____ inches

3. (I) __3__ inches   Add 3" to the length of <u>each</u>
                          <u>panel</u> for handling ease.

Note: I usually do not subtract for doors and windows
unless there are many and they are large and occupy
space nearly floor to ceiling. You will have some extra
fabric pieces, but they are great for pillows, etc.

4. Total the above measurements.

   (G) _____ inches
   (H) _____ inches
   (I) _____ inches

   (J) _____ Panel Length in Inches

STEP THREE – CONVERTING PANEL LENGTHS TO YARDS

1. (J) × (F) = (K) Total Inches   Multiply panel length (J)
              Needed   times the number of panels
                                      (F), to determine total
                                      inches of fabric needed.

2.   (L) No. of Yards   Divide the total length (K)
      36" ⟌ (K) total inches   by 36" to determine the
                                       yards of fabric needed.

8

It is a good idea to add a yard or two for leeway, and more if you are planning to make curtains, shades, etc.

See p. 31 for how to measure for shirred walls.

AS YOU BEGIN—Tips & Techniques

PLUMB LINES

Establishing a plumb line as you proceed along the wall will help keep the fabric panels straight.

Attach a string to a plumb bob or heavy object such as a pair of scissors. Rub the cord with chalk and attach it to the top of the wall along the edge of the first panel. Hold the weight at the baseboard and snap the line against the wall. The vertical mark is your guide.

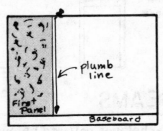

Note: You do not have to chalk the string, but it is very helpful. You may just hang the line along the panel and leave it as you work. I plumb each panel I apply. This assures getting each panel straight and not stretching it.

PUSH PINS

Push pins hold the fabric in place while you get it straight, and as you apply it to the wall. When you work alone with starch or paste methods, it helps to move the pins down the wall as you work. (Keeps the fabric from coming down on your head if you tug too hard on occasion.)

Fabric Panel

Note: A strip of double face tape may work if walls are too hard for push pins.

*I like the long point (5/8") pins from stationery stores.

WHERE DO I START?

If your fabric has a design that distinctly requires centering, begin in the center of the most conspicuous wall, and work in both directions.

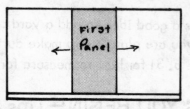

Otherwise it is easiest to
pick the least conspicuous
corner or area and begin
there. Thus if you wrap the
fabric around the room returning to the starting point, this
will be the least noticed spot to finish off the last seam,
which usually will not match.

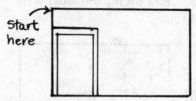
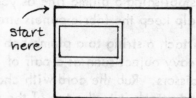

SEAMS

Techniques covered below relate to DAMP methods--glue,
paste, starch, etc. Seam techniques for stapled fabrics
appear later in the chapter. (See pp. 20-21)

I have found essentially three ways of handling seams--
OVERLAPPING, OVERLAP AND CUT, AND BUTTED.
You can discover which is best and easiest for a fabric by
including a seam or two in a test sample.

Overlapping   (The Landlord Seam)

With firm lightweight (i.e. chintz, broadcloth, etc.) fabric
overlapping may be satisfactory. I personally prefer methods
with no lump or ridge at seams. However, in apartments or
rentals this may be the best method since it makes no marks
on the walls. It has one other advantage--since the seam
is not cut back to the pattern match, the fabric may be removed from the wall, washed, and used for another project
where seams could then be sewn, lapped and cut, or backtacked.

On most fabrics the design match is printed at or near the
selvage. The seam can be easily overlapped and matched.
On some fabrics the match may be 2" to 3" in from the
edge. Thus to easily overlap a seam, the excess should be

trimmed off leaving about 1/2" overlap byond the match.

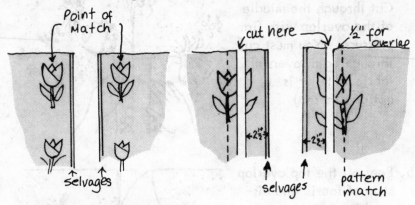

Overlap and Cut

A professional seam that is easy to do. Best for fabrics you can 'see through' while working and fabrics that tend to ravel easily. (This is my favorite method.)

1. If needed, trim off excess fabric to create about 1" of overlap. (see above)

2. Apply fabric to wall being careful to match design. On many lighter fabrics you will be able to see through the top layer while it is wet, thus making it easier to align it with the design beneath. Smooth overlap into place.

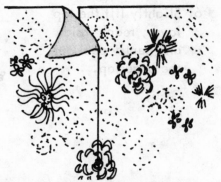

3. Allow seam to 'set' for about a half hour or so before cutting. This allows time for some shrinkage and relaxation. The seam must be cut while it is still damp and flexible, but there will be ample time. Meanwhile you can proceed with succeeding panels.

4. To cut the seam use a SHARP single edge razor blade or one of the 'snap-off' blade trimmers available in wallpaper and art stores. Since only the point is used, you use lots of blades. Discard blades as they dull to prevent 'chewing' the fabric.

11

4. Cont'd.
   Cut through the middle
   of the overlap with firm
   pressure. You must cut
   through both layers of
   fabric. (Ruler is
   optional here.)

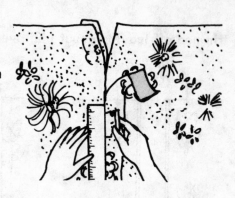

5. Peel off the top overlap
   strip of fabric and discard it.

6. Slightly lift the top
   layer, reach inside
   and gently peel out
   the underlap.

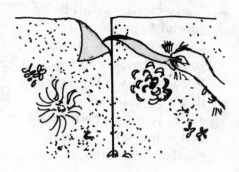

7. Smooth the cut edges to-
   gether--applying a little
   starch if needed.

   Note: If a little shrinkage
   occurs and edges separate
   a bit, apply a little more
   starch and push them back.
   If you can get them to dry
   together, they stay together.

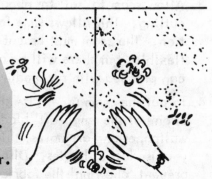

Butted Seam

On occasion I find it best to butt seams together. Fabrics that warrant this treatment include:

-- Fabrics with a white selvage adjacent to the pattern match. Lapping and cutting this fabric is difficult since

it is unlikely you can overlap and cut without some of the white selvage left in the seam finish.

-- Fabrics dark in color or heavy enough that you can't see through them when they are wet.

1. Apply the fabric panel to the wall following the plumb line to keep the edges even and straight.

2. Using a metal edge ruler and a SHARP razor blade, trim off the selvage and lap through the center of the design match. (By cutting the strip after applying to the wall, there is less chance of raveling the edge.)

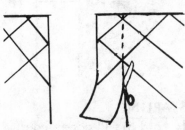

3. With SHARP scissors, care- fully cut the excess lap from the next adjoining panel. Be sure to cut right at the pattern match.

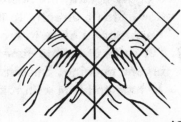

4. Butt cut edges together. Match design, working and smoothing fabric into place. Then work you way across the rest of the panel.

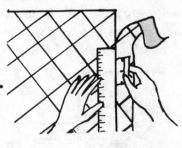

RAVELINGS

Ravelings may occur along cut
edges. DO NOT PULL THEM.
Cut them off with a sharp razor
blade held firmly at the seam.

GOING AROUND AND OVER
Doors, Windows, etc.

Leave the fabric uncut as long as possible if it handles con-
veniently. Smooth it up to the opening and secure with
push pins as needed. Cut away excess fabric leaving about
I" overlapping the frame. Clip at corner to fit fabric.

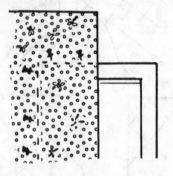
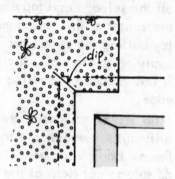

STAPLING

1. Fold the I" edge under so it is fitted
   snuggly against the doorway or window. Staple directly to the wall.
   Keep staples close to the frame, <u>OR</u>
2. Put strips of double-faced tape
   around opening. Smooth fabric onto tape and trim with razor blade, <u>OR</u>

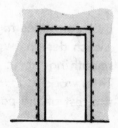

3. Use upholsterer's tape and finish off with brads as described on page 21.

STARCH OR PASTE

Smooth fabric up close to framework; allow fabric to dry completely. Use a SHARP razor blade and metal edge rule to cut cleanly near frame. Peel away the fabric strip.

OPEN DOORWAYS OR ARCHES

1. First paint the inside of the doorway (if needed). Bring paint onto wall 1/2" so you get a clean line when fabric is trimmed. Apply fabric, overlapping doorway slightly. Mark edge of doorway with chalk or pencil. Use SHARP blade and metal edge guide to trim fabric 1/8" to 1/4" from doorway edge, OR use SHARP scissors to trim fabric.

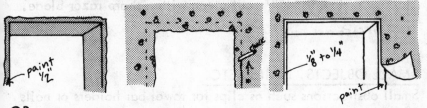

OR

2. Wrap fabric onto inside of recess 1/2". Clip curve and smooth to fit. Cut and apply a <u>matching</u> strip of fabric 1/4" narrower than doorway, and as long as 1/2 the opening.

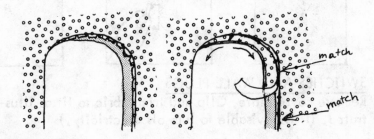

LARGE PROJECTIONS

When an object projects several inches from the wall, it is difficult to apply fabric over it first. You may need to make a clean cut from the nearest or least conspicuous edge. Then cut away excess fabric. When two or more objects are adjacent in

15

the center of a fabric panel,
cut through the shortest distance to that object and
clip around it, leaving an
overlap of about an inch.
Make slashes (see below) to
help fabric fit around the
object.

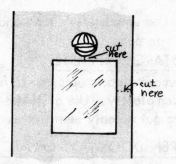

To wrap fabric around a pipe or round fixture make a clean
cut through the fabric from either the shortest or least conspicuous edge. Then make a series
of slashes and fit the fabric around
the object. When fabric is dry,
cut clean with a sharp razor blade.

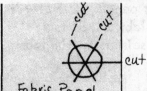

Fabric Panel

SMALL OBJECTS, NAILS, ETC.
Small obstructions such as clips for towel bar holders or nails
for pictures may be covered over. Then take a razor blade
and slit the fabric, allowing the object to slip through.

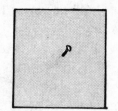

SWITCHES AND WALL PLUGS
Remove cover plate. Clip and trim fabric to fit as illustrated. (It is advisable to turn off electricity.)

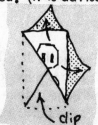

clip

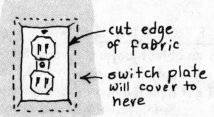

cut edge
of fabric

switch plate
will cover to
here

COVERED SWITCHPLATES

A professional touch is evident when you cover **switchplates** with matching fabric. Cut a piece of fabric to match the wall area and plate. Glue fabric to face of plate, check alignment, let dry. Then clip, wrap and glue to back side.

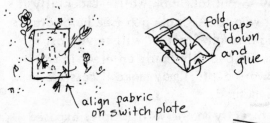

align fabric on switch plate

fold flaps down and glue

CORNERS

Trimming corners at ceiling and baseboard will be easier if you make vertical clips in the fabric as you apply it. When completely dry--trim with razor blade, cutting off two separate strips.

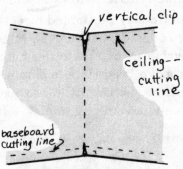

vertical clip

ceiling-- cutting line

baseboard cutting line

For outside exposed corners trim 1/8" to 1/4" from corner to prevent raveling. Use selvage if possible.

⅛"-¼" from corner

SOFFITS

The space between kitchen cupboards and ceiling is an easy and obvious place for fabric. Be sure to measure soffit height

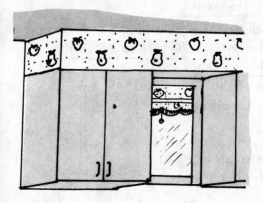

in several places before you begin, as soffits are often very uneven.

Cut the bottom edge of fabric smoothly with scissors, allowing 1" at ceiling to be trimmed later, when fabric is dry. Or cut fabric to fit exactly and staple or starch in place.

17

WAYS TO FABRIC WALLS

Stapling

Stapling is an easy way to put fabric on walls--especially if walls are sheet rock or wood. A staple gun (see hardware) is a handy tool, and a lightweight 'tacker' will serve most all your needs. If walls are especially hard, an electric staple gun (available in hardware depts.) may make it possible to attach fabric with this method.

Fabric may be stapled directly to the wall (staples exposed or covered); backtacked to conceal staples; or applied to furring strips. The latter help conceal rough or uneven walls, or make it possible to staple to plaster or concrete. You will be suprised at the amount of texture that can be effectively covered by staples. Try a test sample.

Note: Remember--a coat of paint will fill old staple holes--so fabric now, paint later.

If selvages are much more firmly woven than the body of the fabric, remove or clip them, thus preventing drag lines later if selvages remain taut while fabric relaxes. Another cause of drag or pull lines in stapled fabric can result from fabric printed off grain. Since the pattern must be placed straight on the wall, the grainline may be distorted and cause ripples. Select and check fabric carefully.

STAPLING DIRECTLY TO THE WALL

1. Cut fabric panels the desired length plus one inch on the top and one inch on the bottom. Be sure to match the pattern brfore you cut each panel.
2. Determine the position of the first panel and establish a plumb line. (p. 9).
3. Start at the top. Use push pins or double face tape to hold fabric.
4. Staple at top every 2" -3" close

18 to the edge.

5. When fabric is secure, pull at bottom opposite each staple at top, keeping fabric taut and smooth, but not over-stretched.

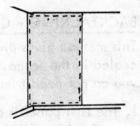

6. Staple one side, then the other.

7. Push pin and overlap the next panel flat (A) or folding under (B), staple seam. Staple top, bottom, and side. Continue with succeeding panels.

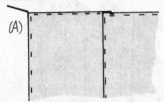

(A)

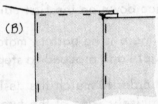

(B)

8. Cut off excess at ceiling and floor with a sharp razor blade and a metal edge ruler as a guide.

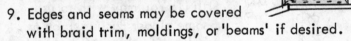

fold under & staple

← staple raw edge flat

fold under & staple

Note: If you prefer, you may turn edges at top, bottom, and sides under and staple them in place.

9. Edges and seams may be covered with braid trim, moldings, or 'beams' if desired.

For beams sand and paint boards. Position ceiling strip first, then floor, with vertical strips last. Boards may be flat to the wall or can stand away, depending on the desired effect.

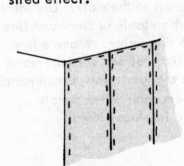

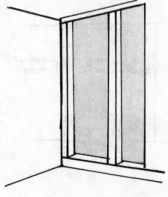

BACKTACKING – CONCEALED SEAMS

This method gives professional looking walls with staples concealed in the seams. It is neat, fast, and economical since you do not need trim or molding to cover seams.

1. The first panel is applied the same as in the previous directions (steps 1 thru 6) for applying fabric directly to the wall.

2. The second panel is positioned face down on the first panel.

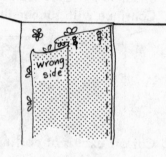

3. If there is no pattern match, staple and proceed to step 4.

   In order to match the design precisely, one of the two techniques that follow can help to simplify things.

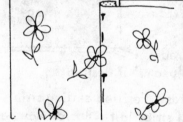

a. Slip straight pins into the fold to hold design correctly. Then fold fabric back carefully and staple.

> HINT: You may wish to use some zipper Basting Tape to help align the pattern match.

OR

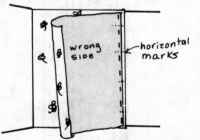

b. You may prefer to 'key' the design before applying panels to the wall. Lay fabric out on table or floor and line up the design. Make a few horizontal and vertical marks on the fabric so you can match them again when panels are in place on wall.

4. To make a firm edge that will distribute tension evenly, place a piece of upholsterer's tape (see hardware) along the seam and staple it in place.

5. Pull the panel back against the edge of the upholsterer's tape and staple it in place.

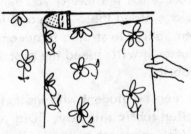

6. Finish ceiling and wall edges by cutting cleanly with a sharp razor blade and metal edge ruler as guide, unless you have been folding the top and bottom edges under as you went along.

7. Continue to backtack the panels as you work your way around the room.

8. At the last edge fold the fabric over a piece of upholsterer's tape and fasten the edge up snugly to the wall by pounding 3/4" wire brads (see hardware) in place.

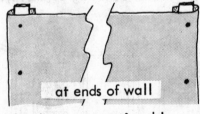

at ends of wall

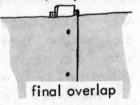

final overlap

9. If brads are not noticeable, pound them flat. If they show, you can conceal them: 1) Pound in until about 1/16" is exposed. 2) Take a couple of pins and lift and pick at the threads until they open and 'swallow' the brad. 3) Pound the brad in flat.

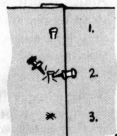

1.

2.

3.

21

SEAMED PANELS

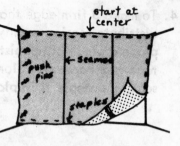

It is possible to seam fabric lengths together before applying to a wall. The main difficulties are getting good even tension on the fabric and the size of the panel thus created.

To combat the former you may want to staple the fabric in place along the ceiling and let it hang for 24 hours to allow the fabric to stretch to accommodate its weight. To ease the latter it will speed the process to have help in applying the fabric.

I recall a student who indicated she and her husband had applied fabric this way. "Did you find it easy?" I inquired. "No, it almost ended in divorce," she laughed, "but it looked great when it was finished."

FURRING STRIPS

Furring strips are thin wood strips, which can be purchased at lumber yards, or you can saw a board into thin (3/8" or 1/4" thick) strips on a table saw. They are used as a 'buffer' so fabric can be stretched and stapled, thus allowing rough or uneven walls to be covered. They can also be attached to concrete or hard plaster walls (with nails or paneling adhesive).

1. Apply furring strips to the wall along ceiling, floor, each side of a corner, and vertically where seams will lie. Outline doors and windows.

2. Attach fabric to furring strips by one of the methods described above under stapling.

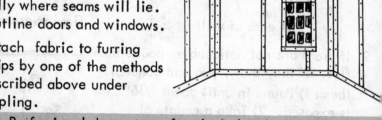

Note: Professional decorators often 'upholster' a wall by stapling heavy flannel, or 1/2" thick fireproof dacron to the furring strips first. Fabric panels are then seamed and stapled to the wall. Trim edges with gimp or double welting.

22

Starching

There is no doubt this is my favorite method. It is a bit messy during the process, but it does a great job and has many advantages:

- starching leaves fewer bubbles in the fabric application than cellulose wallpaper paste
- starched fabric can be peeled off the wall when you want a change, the fabric can be washed and used again
- a simple sponging with soap and water, spot lifter, or cleaning fluid helps keep the fabric clean
- walls don't have to be sized or prepared as long as they can withstand moisture (untreated plaster or drywall should be sealed)

WHAT WORKS?

Chintz works superbly with starch, especially when it is 100% cotton. Other cottons and blends of similar weight and type also work very well.

I have used all-cotton chintz in a bathroom (a steamy one with no fan and smooth enameled walls) and have even starched a Scotchguarded fabric to a kitchen soffit. It is gratifying to have former students report good results with many types of fabrics. One recently reported putting a ZePel treated fabric in a non-steamy bath, but I think the award for daring goes to the girl who starched burlap over flocked foil wallpaper in her dining room!

The best advice about what fabrics and surfaces will work is TRY A TEST SAMPLE. That will tell you more than any amount of guesswork. Relax and experiment. Latex, enamel, paneling, glass, plastic, tile, wood, concrete, metal can all be covered.

ABOUT STARCH

Always use liquid starch--not spray starch! I usually use premixed liquid, undiluted from the bottle. The common brands are usually pink or blue in color--but this does not affect the color of the fabric. On occasion I have mixed powdered starch with water to a consistency of medium white sauce.

23

CHECK THE LABEL

Check to see if the starch contains a mildew inhibitor, especially if you plan to put fabric in a bath or other potentially damp area. The addition of a small amount of disinfectant would be wise, or you can purchase a product from wallpaper stores that will do the job.

Note: Some starch contains salt, which can cause pitting or rusting of scissors, razor blades, and metal if starch is not rinsed off as you work. (Use care near hinges, door stops, formica trim, etc.) Try to use aluminum nails for hanging pictures in steamy areas like bathrooms.

STARCHING A WALL

Read directions carefully, including seams, openings, and edge techniques detailed earlier in the chapter.

1. Wash the wall if it is very soiled or to remove greasy film.

2. Cut panels the desired length plus 1" on the top and the bottom. Be sure to match the design before you cut each panel. (Trim off the firmly woven portion of the selvage if it has been pulled or distorted in the printing process.)

3. If the pattern match if more than 1" from the edge, trim off excess leaving no more than 1" overlap. (see p. 10)

4. Determine placement of first panel; establish a plumb line. Protect floor with plastic.

    Note: Because of the stretchy nature of some fabrics, it is a good idea to plumb each panel.

5. Pour starch into pan. Use sponge about 1" thick. Saturate sponge with starch, apply liberally to the wall for the first few feet.

Note: You may prefer to use a paint roller to apply the starch both to the wall and top of fabric. It causes less distortion with some prints, is fast and easy. A sponge can be used for bubbles and small areas.

6. Smooth fabric into place at the top of the wall, leaving about 1" to be trimmed later. Use push pins to hold fabric temporarily as you work your way down the panel, adding starch underneath by lifting the panel when needed.

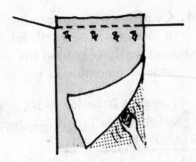

7. Now apply starch to the top of the panel, brushing and smoothing the fabric in place to remove bubbles and wrinkles. Be sure the starch penetrates the fabric evenly. This step creates a smooth application and soil resistant finish.

Note: Do not be suprised if some bubbles are evident when the fabric has dried. Simply soak them with starch and smooth them out. (This is most likely in medium and heavier fabrics.)

8. Work your way down the panel--continuing to sponge starch onto the wall, smoothing the fabric, and applying more starch.

9. Position the second panel, matching the design along the edge. Treat the seam by overlapping, lapping and cutting, or butting. (See seams starting on p. 10)

10. Seams are cut while fabric is damp. However, the fabric should be cut at the floor, ceiling, and around doors and windows when it has DRIED COMPLETELY. It will then cut clean--like paper. Any shrinkage will have occurred before you trim.

Note: If you make an accidental cut while trimming, starch it back. Let dry. Trim.

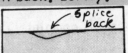

splice back

ceiling

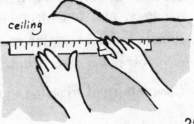

25

11. Continue with succeeding panels. If you are wrapping two or more walls, smooth fabric into the corner and onto the next wall, plumbing the edge before you start the next panel. Smooth and tug fabric into line if needed.

Note: It is easier to wipe up excess starch from ceiling, baseboards, or window frames as you go--before it dries.

REMOVING FABRIC

When you decide to remove fabric from a wall if you move or re-decorate, peel one corner loose, then gently begin to peel the fabric panel off. If the fabric is holding very snugly and you are concerned that it may pull some paint, just moisten it with a damp sponge and continue to peel it loose. When the fabric is damp, it will strip smoothly and evenly.

Cellulose Wallpaper Paste

Non-staining cellulose wallpaper paste (wheat paste can stain fabrics and is difficult to remove) can be used for fabric. Make a test patch, as the holding power varies with fabric and wall surface. However, fabric usually strips off easily with little or no residue. In many cases the fabric can be washed and the paste residue removed. Shiny, slick walls may need to be sized first, but most require no preparation.

1. Prepare wall if needed, and cut panels of fabric. Match design before cutting. Plumb the wall.

2. Mix paste following package directions, and brush or roll directly on the wall. Apply paste the width of the panel and 3 to 4 feet deep.

3. Press fabric into place and smooth it with hands and a smooth object such as a wallpaper brush, or roller. Leave 1" at ceiling and baseboard and around doors, windows, etc. to be trimmed away later when dry.

4. Handle seams according to chosen method. (see p. 10)

5. Wipe off seams, baseboards, etc.

6. Complete final trimming when fabric is completely dry.

Vinyl Wallpaper Paste

Pre-mixed vinyl wallpaper paste has excellent holding power for fabrics--especially heavier types.   It is also the most expensive method, but very easy to apply.

As always, make a test sample to determine holding power and stripability. Follow directions for cellulose paste. Be careful to keep the paste off the surface of the fabric.

Gluing

White glues such as Elmers or Sobo can be used to apply fabric. It is a fairly permanent method with excellent holding power on most surfaces, but could remove some paint when stripped off.

1. Prepare the fabric panels and plumb the wall.

2. Dilute glue--one to one with water. Apply as for wallpaper paste method. Roll the glue mixture on with a paint roller, or apply with a paint brush.

3. Smooth fabric into place, brush and smooth out wrinkles and bubbles.

4. Treat seams with your choice of method. (see p. 10)

5. Wash up spills or drips as you go. Trim at ceiling, floor, windows, etc. when fabric is <u>almost</u> dry. Sponge off any excess glue mixture before it dries.

Fabric Wrapped Panels

Picture a wall with a window on each end and empty space between, or a small wall space that you would like to cover 'temporarily' with fabric. A panel that fits the space floor to ceiling can be wrapped in fabric and attached to the wall (toe-nailed) with finishing nails. If the panel is cut the right size, it can often be slipped into place between floor and ceiling without the need of nails.

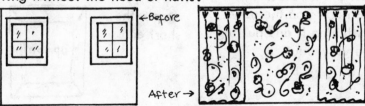

←Before

After →

Using this panel technique you can wrap a wall or an entire room with only an occasional nail needed to hold the panels in place. This is a good method for rough or textured walls.

You may even find it easier to work with fabric in this way since the panels are wrapped while they are down flat, and then set in place.

Damaged or low quality wall paneling is inexpensive and can be cut to fit around windows, doors, etc. Foam board (see hardware) would be light, easy to handle, and can be cut easily with an exacto knife. Upson board (see hardware) 1/4" thick works as well, but must be sawed. Both of the latter are more expensive than paneling.

Vinyl Wrapped Panels

Should you desire to wrap <u>vinyl</u> snugly to a panel such as upson board, a simple technique will enable you to get it stretched really smooth.

Note: Do not attempt this with foam board.

1. First staple the vinyl along one long edge of the panel.

2. Then lift the panel and slip a rug tube, or plastic pipe under the panel making it bow slightly.

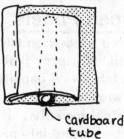

Cardboard tube

3. Pull the second long edge snugly over the panel and staple.

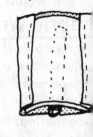

4. Pull the tube out and push down on the panel, flattening it and pulling the vinyl taut.

5. Finally, staple the short ends.

staples

28

Changeable Panels

A unique system of panels can be built and assembled in such a way that the upper fabric-wrapped panel can be changed by lifting it out, recovering, and slipping it back in place. This method also helps conceal rough or damaged walls.

1. First apply sheetrock to the lower half of the wall.

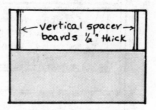

2. Then apply vertical boards 3" to 4" wide and the same thickness as the sheetrock. (Boards may be painted or stained.)

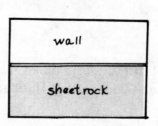

3. Then place horizontal boards across the verticals. This leaves 1/2" space under the board.

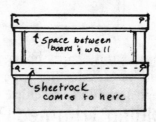

4. Cut sheetrock wide enough to fit between the verticals (A), and high enough to sit on the bottom wall of sheetrock and go up under the top horizontal by about 1/2" (B).

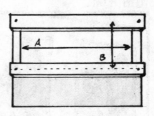

5. Wrap and staple fabric around the panel. Staple a couple of straps made from canvas or vinyl to enable you to lift the panels in and out.

front

Back of sheetrock panel

6. Lift the fabric panel into place and your wall is finished!

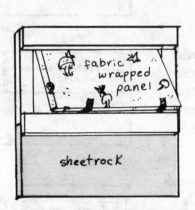

fabric wrapped panel

sheetrock

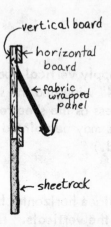

vertical board

horizontal board

fabric wrapped panel

sheetrock

Note: Upson board, homosote (see hardware), or foam board could be used for the upper half of the wall. They are lighter and less likely to chip.

Molding Trimmed Panels

Apply fabric to wall, then outline panels with wood molding or braid trim.

Also try fabric panels on doors, cupboards, drawers, etc.
If molding is already in place on the object, you may remove it, and apply fabric, then replace molding. Or
you can cut fabric to fit inside molding and use wallpaper
paste or starch to apply.

Shirred Walls

A sumptuous wall treatment is achieved by shirring or gathering fabric on a wall or an entire room.

While requiring a great deal of fabric, the installation of this
method is relatively easy. Fabric panels need not be seamed
together since the edges can easily be hidden in the gathers.

Sheets are a natural for this method because of their economical width.

FIGURING YARDAGE

1. width of wall _____ x fullness desired* _____ = _____
                                                      Total Width

    *2x is fairly standard, many
     prefer 2 1/2x, 3x is quite full

2. Total width _____ ÷ width of fabric _____ = _____
                                                   No. of
                                                   Panels

3. Floor to ceiling measurement _____ inches
   Allowance for top and bottom
   hems   + 6 inches

   Take up when rods are inserted in casings   + 1 inches
                                 _____
              Panel Length _____ inches

4. Panel length _____ x number of panels _____ = _____
                                                     Yardage
                                                     in inches

5. Yardage in inches _____ ÷ 36 " = _____ No. of
                                             yards needed

31

FOR SHEETS

1. width of wall _____ in. x fullness desired _____ = _____ in. Total
   Width

2. total width _____ in. ÷ width of sheet _____ in. =
   you will use

   No. of
   sheets

PREPARING FABRIC

Turn hem edge under 3". Press.
Turn raw edge under 1/2" and
machine stitch hem in place.

Run another row of stitches
across the panel 1 1/2" from
fold.

Repeat at bottom.

Note: For sheets--try to use
the stitched hems where
possible.

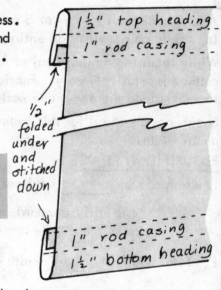

1½" top heading
1" rod casing

½" folded under and stitched down

1" rod casing
1½" bottom heading

INSTALLATION

1. Cafe curtain brackets and rods
   are installed at intervals
   along ceiling and floor.
   Fabric panels are shirred
   onto rods. Hang rods in
   brackets and adjust the
   gathers for evenness.

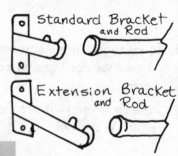

Standard Bracket
and Rod

Extension Bracket
and Rod

NOTE: Cup hooks and dowels
or rods may be used as above.
It is a more economical method.

OR

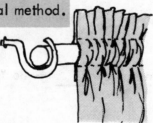

2. Prepare fabric as above. Thread half round molding (from lumberyard) through the hem casings. Adjust the gathers evenly, then nail the top molding to the wall at about 12" intervals with finishing nails. Pull the fabric taut, adjust gathers and nail bottom molding. This creates a very neat installation, but more permanent than cafe rods.

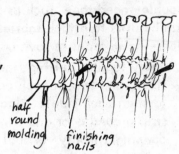

half round molding   finishing nails

3. Fabric may be attached directly to wall with staples after fabric has been shirred with shirring tape.
Stitch hems and tape as indicated. Pull cords to shirr fabric. Staple to wall.

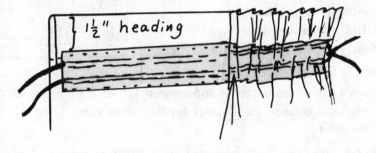

1½" heading

Your shirred wall is sure to please!

Double-Faced Tape

Double-faced tape such as masking tape or carpet-type tape can be used to attach fabric to walls. (Be sure to read directions--some tapes remove paint and even wood when removed.)

1. Apply tape at ceiling line, floor, and two in each corner (one on each side). Place a strip around door and window openings. Apply vertical strips where edges of each fabric length will meet on the wall. (Edges of fabric should butt, not overlap.) Do not remove the protective covering strip at this time.

2. Starting in one corner at ceiling, remove paper from adhesive for one width of fabric.

3. Smooth fabric over tape.

4. Remove cover from corner tape about 12" at a time; smooth fabric over adhesive. Repeat for the other side, keeping fabric taut.

5. Stretch and press onto bottom tape a little at a time, lining up weave or pattern. Trim surplus later.

6. Repeat with second fabric length. Match pattern on seams and butt edges of second fabric length to first panel.

7. Repeat around doors and windows, trimming away surplus fabric. The tape will hold down the raw edges.

8. When all surfaces are covered, trim excess with sharp blade

Fabric Ceilings

Fabric may be applied to ceilings by a variety of methods. Whichever you choose, it will probably be necessary to have help in applying the fabric overhead.

Review the directions for figuring yardage, being sure to determine which way fabric will run before measuring.

DIRECT APPLICATION

1. Smooth Firm Ceilings
Fabric may be applied by starch, glue, wallpaper paste, or staples. Follow directions for walls.

2. Textured or Soft Ceilings
Apply furring strips as on page 21, then staple fabric to furring strips.

SUSPENDED APPLICATION

Suspended fabric not only creates a very special effect in a room, it can conceal ceiling height, or rough and uneven ceilings.

Attach dowels or cafe curtain rods to wall. Use the curtain brackets, cup hooks, screw hooks or screw eyes to hold the rods. Run rods along the center of the ceiling, too. Drape fabric across the rod, or run the rod through a casing stitched in the fabric.

Idea: Fabric can be draped and stapled directly to beams or open rafter ceiling. Low voltage lighting above a patchwork ceiling gives stained glass effect.

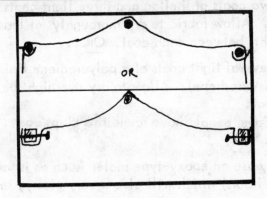

Fabric Floors

For an exciting and different effect--fabric a floor! The resulting application will be quite permanent, but could be covered with carpeting or new floor covering at a later date.

The floor can withstand a great deal of abuse, if it is prepared properly. (One couple even had fabric applied to the floor in their children's playroom!)

1. Measure floor and determine fabric needs.

2. Clean the floor completely; use a grease remover (trisodium-phosphate), and be sure it is vaccuumed well.

3. Measure and determine center of the floor and mark location for first panel.

4. Center the first panel and apply to floor with starch or white glue diluted with a little water. Use butt technique on seams. Be sure to cut off all ravelings carefully with a sharp razor blade before they dry.

5. Allow fabric to dry completely, then--

   a. apply two coats of shellac and three light coats of varnish. Allow fabric to dry thoroughly (at least overnight) between each coat. OR....

   b. Apply several light coats of a polyurethane finish (such as Varathane). Allow to dry overnight between each coat.
   Note: Some people have found this chips easier than above method. OR...

   c. You may use an epoxy-type sealer (such as is used for gym floors) which will give a very glossy, smooth finish.

CORNICES / CANOPIES

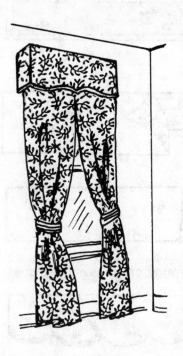

Cornices are solid (usually wood) frames. They are padded, covered with fabric, and suspended over windows. Valances are of soft or slightly stiffened fabric and are suspended in a similar manner. A canopy may often be an enlarged cornice, or valance. So when searching for canopy ideas for a bedroom—consider cornice techniques.

There are numerous ways to construct a cornice, canopy or valance. One method may be a bit easier than another because of the materials you have on hand, your past experience with tools, or the construction of your home or apartment.

Hopefully you will find among the many ideas that follow, one or more that particularly suits your needs.

Stiffened Buckram

A stiffened 'buckram' such as Conso's Permette can make a flexible yet sturdy cornice or valance that can be mounted on a curtain rod or dowel. Permette is available by the yard in 11" and 36" widths and is washable and cleanable.

Cut Permette strip the desired length. (Add for side returns if box cornice.)

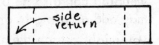

side return

Stitch a 2" strip of twill tape or drapery lining 1/2" from top and side edges to form casing for rod.

Wrap padding, such as poly-ester fleece, around the Permette. Stitch by machine, taking care not to stitch the rod pocket closed.

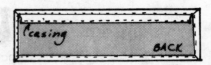

Cut fabric 3" longer and 2" wider than Permette. Lay RIGHT side of fabric on the WRONG side of Permette. Stitch 1/2" seam.

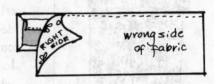

Flip fabric to right side and finish sides and bottom by hand.

Note: Permette may be cut into fancy or ornamental shapes and covered in same manner. To trim bottom edge--cut with scissors, stitch on machine and glue trim to cover stitches.

The only complaint I have ever heard about this method is that across very wide windows, the cornice sometimes tends to 'dip inward' at the center. Thus some type of brace or stiffener may need to be devised.

OTHER STIFFENERS

Buckram, iron-on Detail Pelomite, commercial roller shade backing such as Tran Lam, or fabric bonded with fusible webbing can also be used to create stiffened cornices. You may add a casing in order to use them on curtain rods, or you might attach them to a mounting board.

Mounting Board

A board fastened above a window with angle irons, which are anchored to wall studs, can form the base for a variety of different cornice treatments.

The board must be wide enough and long enough to clear the window treatment beneath. Then--

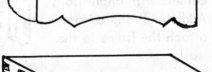

Fold the top edge of the cornice over the board and staple in place, OR--

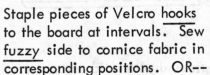

Staple pieces of Velcro hooks to the board at intervals. Sew fuzzy side to cornice fabric in corresponding positions. OR--

Pre-shrink snap tape, then staple half to mounting board, sew half to top of cornice. OR--

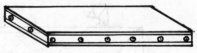

Pre-shrink hook and eye tape. Staple hooks to board, sew eyes to top of cornice. OR--

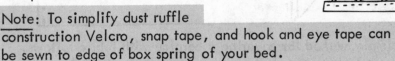

Note: To simplify dust ruffle construction Velcro, snap tape, and hook and eye tape can be sewn to edge of box spring of your bed.

Pound U-shaped screen staples into edge of board at intervals that correspond to the spacing of pleats on a valance. Be sure a pleat is positioned on the corners of the valance. OR--

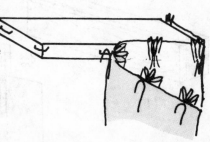

Pad and fabric wrap a 'frame' of upson board, foam board, or

cardboard. Attach the frame
to the mounting board.

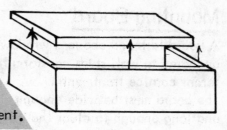

Note: A mounting board cornice provides a built-in dust
cover for your window treatment.

Box Cornices

These can be constructed
of boards secured at
corners with angle irons.
Additional angle irons
attach the frame to the
wall.

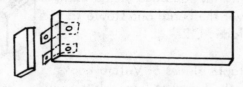

When a box-like cornice is constructed with solid dust-cover
top, angle irons are usually attached to the top.

A simple method for covering a cornice with fabric follows.
Try cutting a pattern from brown paper first, if not familiar
with cutting and wrapping techniques.

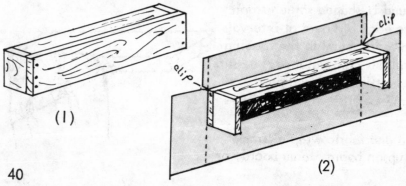

(1)

(2)

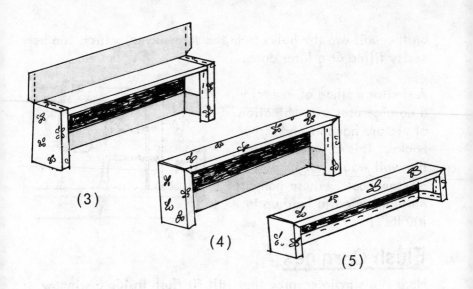

(3)

(4)

(5)

A Cardboard Cornice

A sturdy piece of cardboard can be cut to size, then scored with a utility knife and bent to form a light-weight cornice.

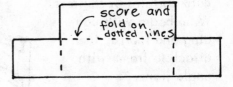

score and fold on dotted lines

Mounting Ideas

Light weight cornices from cardboard or foam board can be attached to walls with ordinary straight pins driven

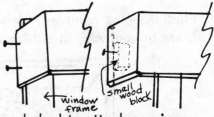

window frame

small wood block

in with a hammer. If there is no 'edge' to attach cornice, a small block of wood can be fastened to the wall first. The cornice can then be glued or tacked to the block.

An easy cornice mounting consists of screw eyes, which are fastened to the window frame, and screw hooks which are positioned on the cornice. Thus the cornice can be lifted on and off for cleaning, and the only marks

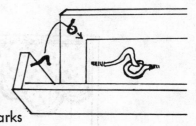

41

on the wall are the holes from the screw eyes, which can be easily filled at a later date.

A similar method of mounting a cornice uses a combination of picture hangars and screw hooks. This is useful where the wall would not support a screw hook. These hangars are calibrated to hold up to 100 lbs. !

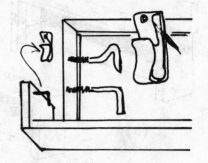

Flush Cornices

Here is a simple cornice that will fit flush inside a window frame to coordinate with roller shade, venetian blind or cafe curtains or shutters.
Wrap board with padding and fabric, then attach to frame with angle irons.

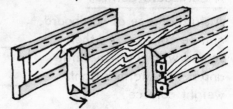

Flush mounted cornices may be mounted inside a window frame or doorway, or outside reaching edge to edge.

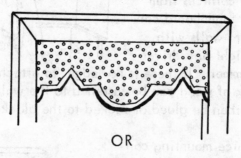

OR

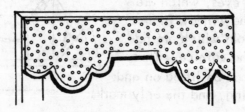

These cornices can be made from cardboard, upson board, or foam board (see hardware). They make light weight, but sturdy cornices.

Foam board can be cut with a razor blade, utility knife, or exacto knife, and even with an electric slicing knife!

Upson board, like wood, must be sawed into shape.

To mount the flush cornice made from one of the light weight materials attach small wood blocks inside the window recess with glue or nails. Then fasten the cornice to the blocks with foam tape (the type used on mirror tiles) or straight pins which can be pounded in with a hammer. If your windows have ornamental wood framing, there may be a small 'lip' for the cornice to rest on. Then pins can be pounded into the 'lip'.

NOTE: Cornices not only conceal window treatment hardware and give a decorative touch, they can help save energy, too.

Canopies

A simple canopy over a bed can be obtained by stapling fabric to the wall, up and over a 1" x 6" board covered or painted to match. Trim is glued or stapled to hide the angle irons.   OR--

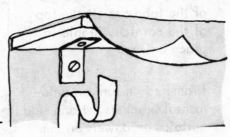

The fabric can be wrapped and stapled in place after being brought up the wall, covering the angle irons.

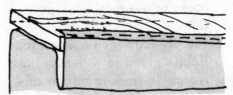

Curtain rods or drapery poles may create a canopy effect. Suspend them from the ceiling or toggle bolt them directly to the ceiling.

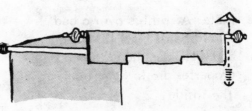

The simplest canopy is obtained by stapling fabric directly to the wall and out onto the ceiling.

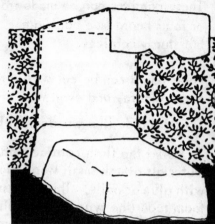

To make a cornice with inside draperies, wrap the cornice with fabric, stapling it along the top edges. Add tubular curtain rod or cup hooks and dowel.

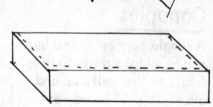

Face and hem a rectangle of the fabric to fit the top of the cornice. Staple in place on top.

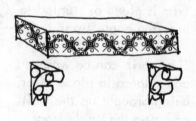

If desired, mount on ornamental brackets. Hang side curtains on dowels on cup hooks or use rods.
OR
Use plywood rectangle on top (fabric glued to underside) and use angle irons to attach cornice to wall.

Note: A cornice over a bed should be at least 12" deep and 4" wider than the bed if draperies are to hang from the inside.

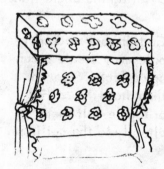

FOLDING SCREENS

Folding screens--a useful decorating tool of the professional decorator--are often overlooked by the do-it-yourselfer. They are simple to make from a variety of methods, and serve many functions.

Consider a folding screen to:
- add interesting angles to a room
- carry color around a corner
- create a focal point behind a sofa
- serve as a room divider between kitchen and dining area
- separate a shared room
- screen off activities such as sewing or laundry
- reverse to show a different color on each side
- conceal needed storage in corners or along walls
- conceal architectural faults or pipes, etc.
- hide a TV set or other furniture
- serve as backdrop for a plant grouping
- serve as a 'mini' privacy screen or shutter

Note: Keep in mind that the same techniques used to cover screens with fabric can also apply to shelves, shutters, wall panels, tables, wall hangings, doors, etc.

Construction

OPEN FRAMEWORK

A lightweight and economical screen can be constructed with 1" x 2" boards (available from lumber supply) which can be secured together with corrugated fasteners or Skotch wood joiners (see hardware). You may prefer to cut your own wood strips from plywood or boards by cutting it to size on a table saw.

Use a carpenter's square (see hardware) to keep work straight, and add short strips for braces at intervals.

A professional effect is achieved by adding thin cardboard, upson board, or poster board to each side of the framework. Tack or glue in place. It gives a firm surface to work on, and prevents light from showing through.

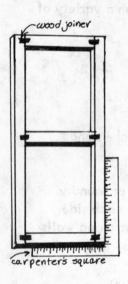
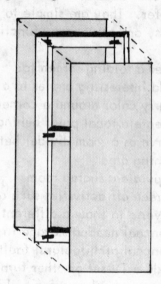

wood joiner

carpenter's square

Wrap panels with fabric, then hinge together using regular hinges or bi-fold hinges. The bi-fold hinge flexes in both directions, giving more versatility to the screen. Look for hinges in hardware stores.

For a special effect you might pad the panels with fleece before wrapping with fabric.

Hint: Bi-fold closet doors make excellent folding screens.

CARDBOARD SCREENS

Inexpensive (about $6) cardboard three-panel folding screens are available in some furniture stores and notions departments. Though they come pre-printed with a design, you can wrap them in fabric by spray gluing or fusing.

An even more economical screen that is totally flexible can

46

be created by obtaining a sturdy cardboard shipping crate.
A carton that once held a refrigerator, freezer, sofa, or
mattress can be cut up into many panels for your screen.
Or cut one edge open, cut off the ends and you have a pre-
folded screen.

To make a paneled
screen cut panels of
desired size.

Lay the panels down
flat, side-by-side
with about 1/2" be-
tween each one.

Cover with webbing,
lay fabric on top
and iron in place on
first panel. Check
spacing between
panels and that
they are even at
top and bottom,
then iron succeed-
ing panels.

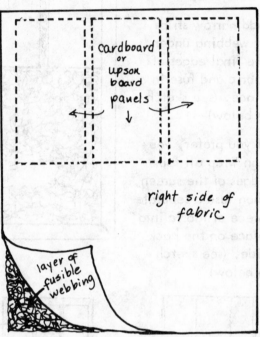

cardboard
or
upson
board
panels

right side of
fabric

layer of
fusible
webbing

Take care to keep the iron on the cardboard. You will be
fusing fabric to your work surface if you go astray.

Note: If you need to splice
on more fabric, overlap the
cut edges with fusible webbing
in between, then press them.

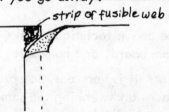

strip of fusible web

Turn the panels right side up on your work surface, smoothing
the fabric and the webbing.

Wrap the top edge over the end of the panels and fuse it
in place. Wrap the side edges over the panels, fuse them
in place.

Fold the bottom edge up, then fold the entire fabric into place on the panels and fuse it down.

Add narrow strips of webbing under the final edges of fabric and fuse in place. (see sketch A below)

If you prefer, you can wrap all four edges of the screen, then fuse a separate piece of fabric into place on the back side. (see sketch B below)

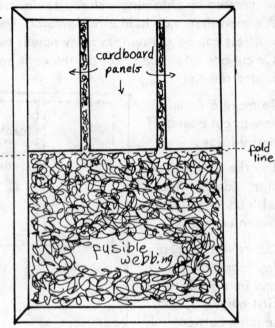

cardboard panels ↓

fold line

fusible webbing

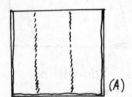

(A)

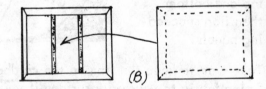

(B)

The above technique works with cardboard, upson board, foam board, and homosote.

Hint: It is very easy to patchwork a screen by cutting fabric pieces and webbing the same size and fusing it randomly in place on the panels. (see chapter on Fusibles)

SLIPCOVERED SCREENS

A fabric slipcover may be sewn to fit over a wood frame or lightweight materials as mentioned above.

Use a tape measure to determine distance around the panel.
Allow distance between panels equal to thickness of panel.

Slip panels into slipcover and whip bottom edge closed.

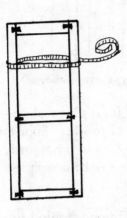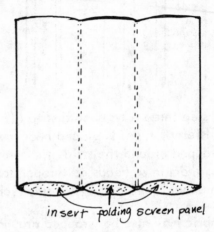

insert folding screen panel

Wrapping Techniques

Cut fabric 2" wider and
longer than board. Wrap
fabric around, stapling it
in place on the back side.
If screen will be against a
wall this is sufficient.

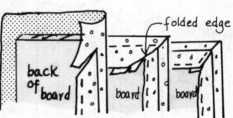

To cover the back, you
can paste fabric over a cut-
to-fit piece of cardboard and
tack to reverse side with
finishing nails or brads, driving them in and working fabric
so head is covered by fabric, but does not go through the
cardboard.

Another method of wrapping a board consists of cutting the
fabric 2" longer on each end than the board, and wide
enough to wrap completely around the board plus 2".

49

Wrap board in following manner:

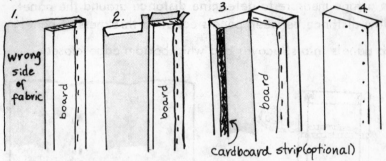

cardboard strip(optional)

In step three a cardboard strip 1/2" wide (or a piece of upholsterer's tape) is placed near raw edge of fabric. Fabric is
wrapped around the strip, then stapled. Or use brads, driving them in so heads go through fabric, but not through the
cardboard. See p. 21 for this technique.

Fabric may also be wrapped around a board and stapled to
the edges. Then a decorative trim is applied by fusing,
gluing, or nailing to hide the staples.

Another way of wrapping wood for firm fabrics that tend not
to ravel follows:

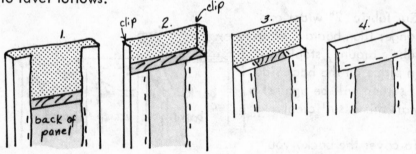

LIQUID STARCH MAKES IT EASY

A quick, easy, and inexpensive way to wrap fabric around
boards, plastic or metal furniture, etc. is to use liquid starch.
Prepare fabric for size of board choosing one of the methods
already described. Using a sponge, apply starch liberally to
one side of the board. Apply fabric and smooth in place.
Adjust and position stripes or design. Then liberally sponge
starch on outside of fabric just placed.
50

Continue your way around the board, sponging on more starch as needed. Allow to dry. You may need to add a bit of glue, fusible web, staples, or brads to the last fold. But the starch will keep the fabric taut.

One of the nicest things about this method is that fabric can be stripped off and changed. Wash the fabric and use it again, the starch won't harm it. Try it on wood, plastic, metal, glass, etc. (Use plastic to protect your work area.)

Spray glues, wallpaper paste, white glues, etc. can also be used to cover folding screens. It will depend on the surface you are covering.

DRAPERIES

Draperies are a popular and classic window treatment. They combine well with curtains and nearly all shade types for special custom effects. They may be used to change mood, apparent size of windows or wall spaces, to block or admit light. Draperies may affect the look and appearance of the outside of your house, too. So this should be considered in the selection of fabric and decision of whether or not to use a lining.

One of the things that makes it difficult to construct large draperies at home is the lack of a work area of sufficient size to really spread out and straighten, cut, and press fabric. You may find it helpful to work at a recreation room or church basement during the initial cutting and pinning stages. If that is not possible--join thousands of us who just 'make do' at home, creating as large an area as possible from plywood and sawhorses, ping pong tables, etc.

THE BASICS

I. MEASURING

Hardware should be installed first, so you can take accurate measurements. Traverse rods are usually installed on the wall at the sides of the window frame, with decorative rods 1" above frame, and conventional rods 2" above the frame.

Rod length is determined by width of glass and stack back needed. Stack back is the area covered by draperies when they are open--uncovering all of the glass. For two-way draw half goes on each side of the window. One-way draw has stack back all on one side. Generally allow an addition of one third the area of the glass for stack back. For very bulky fabrics add an extra inch for each width of fabric.

There are two basic measurements for all draperies:

Finished Width:

The rod length + returns + overlaps = Finished Width

For Standard Rods: Measure end to end + returns + overlaps

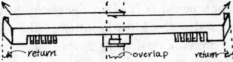

return ⌐overlap return

For Decorative Rods: Measure from just outside brackets + returns + overlaps

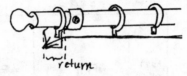

return

For Wood Pole Rods: Measure between brackets. Overlaps are optional

Finished Length:

The distance from the top finished edge of a panel to the bottom finished hem edge is the finished length. This length will be influenced by the type of rod or heading, and whether the drapery stops at apron or floor.

Note: If you do not have an apron on your windows, drapery may stop 4" below the sill.

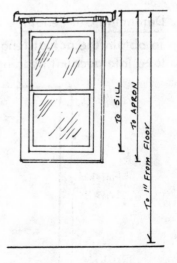

53

2. Determine Total Fabric Width

Use Double Fullness - For pleater tape methods
2-1/2 times Fullness - For standard fabrics
Triple Fullness - For sheer fabrics

To obtain the necessary fullness to allow for gathering and pleating each panel it is often necessary to seam several full widths and part widths together. The illustration is for a one-way draw or stationary drape. Two would be required for a two panel window treatment.

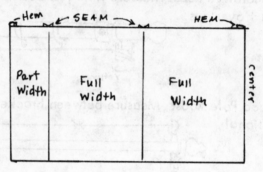

Total Width = Finished Width X Fullness + Side Hems +
Seam Allowances

3. Determine Cut Length

To obtain the actual length to cut each panel you need to take into account headings, hems, and pattern match.

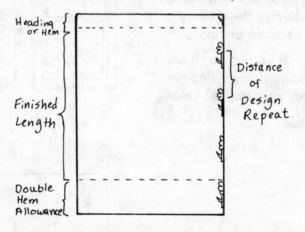

54

A. For Plain Fabrics - or fabrics not requiring pattern match

	_____ " Heading or Casing
+	_____ " Finished Length
+	_____ " Double Bottom Hem
=	_____ " Cut Length for Each Width and Part Width

B. For Fabrics with Pattern Match

Figure length as above. Divide the result in inches by the size of the pattern repeat. If this results in a fraction, order enough extra fabric to get an additional repeat. Most repeats are from 12" to 24". Extra fabric may be used for pillows, placemats, etc.

Example: Cut length = 97" and Pattern Repeat = 12"

Length needed, including hems	=	97"
Pattern repeat	=	12"
Divide 97 by 12	=	8.1
Repeats needed	=	9
Repeats x Size of repeats	=	108" Cut Length Per Width

4. Convert Panel Lengths and Widths to Yards

_____	" Total Cut Length (From A or B above)
X _____	Number of Fabric Widths Needed
= _____	"Total Inches of Fabric Needed ÷ 36" = Total Yards

5. Cut and Prepare Fabric Panels

In order to hang straight and smooth, drapes must be cut on the true lengthwise and crosswise grain of fabric.

Besides matching a patterned fabric at the seams, the design motifs should be placed so the effect will be most pleasing to the eye. It would be ideal to have complete motifs near both top and bottom. When this is not possible, try to position a complete motif near the top on long drapes, where it will be most noticeable, and on the bottom on short drapes. Be sure motifs are placed to match on each pair of panels, and on all windows in the same room.

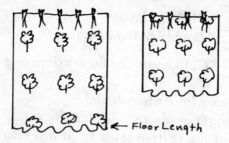

← Floor Length

DRAPES WITH STIFFENER

Determining Yardage: Follow steps on pp. 52-55 and use the following allowances---

    Length: Fabric - Finished length plus 8-1/2"
            Lining - Cut 5-1/2" shorter than cut length of drapery fabric

    Width: Fabric - Allow 2-1/2 times fullness (for standard fabric) plus 4" per panel for side hems and 1/2" for each seam allowance.
           Lining - Cut 6" narrower than drapery fabric

1. Cut, seam and press the drapery panel widths and lining widths. Make a double 4" hem in drapery and double 2" hem in lining.

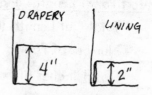

2. Position the lining and drapery with right sides together. Match top and side edges. Lining hem will be 1-1/2" above the drapery hem. Stitch 1/2" side seams.

3. Center the lining on the
   drapery fabric and press
   the seams toward the lining.

   Stitch top edge with a 1/2"
   seam allowance.

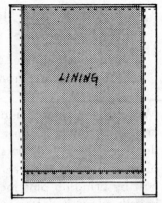

4. Place stiffener on seam
   allowance as shown. Dot
   fabric glue (Wilhold, Quik)
   along the seam allowance.
   Place stiffener in place on
   glue and just above stitching.
   Allow glue to dry.

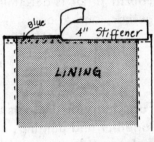

5. Turn entire panel right side
   out like a pillow case.
   (The stiffener will be entirely enclosed within the
   drapery.) Press. Fold
   bottom corners into a 45°
   angle (miter) and tack in
   place.

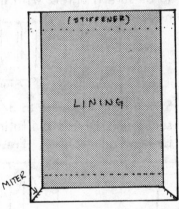

Spacing Pleats

1. The top edge of the panel must be pleated to fit the rod.
   To determine how much fabric must be taken up in pleats:
   A. Total width of panel ___" minus Finished Width (rod,
      returns, overlaps) ___" = Total Inches to Be Pleated

57

B. Total inches to be Pleated ___(A)___" ÷ 4" to 5" (to determine the number of pleats)*= Total Number of Pleats

    *An uneven number of pleats is always preferred so adjust the number from 4 to 5" to obtain an uneven no.

2. Mark off the returns and overlaps on each panel. (If there are none, leave 2" on each end.) Then mark off the pleat depth (4" to 5") at the sides next to the returns. The next pleat is next to the overlaps. Then divide the panel in half by bringing pins together to center the third pleat. Fourth pleat is determined by bringing pleats 1 and 3 together, and so on.

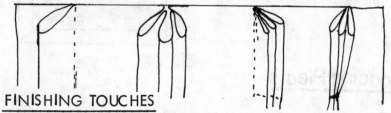

3. Form individual pleats by bringing each pair of markings together and pinning. Remeasure the coverage obtained to be sure it agrees with the finished width. Adjust if needed.

4. Stitch from top edge to 3/4" below heading. Backtack securely. Divide the fullness into thirds. Pin and stitch by hand or machine. Press pleats above stitching.

FINISHING TOUCHES

Draperies and curtains, particularly full length styles will hang better if weights are used at the lower edges. Weights are available in several shapes covered and uncovered. It is advisable to enclose them in the hem when possible. They

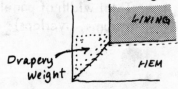

58

may also be covered with a bit of leftover drapery fabric and stitched to the side seam allowance at the hem.

Train the folds in your drapes by opening them and arranging the folds evenly from top to bottom. Tie loosely with several strips of cords or fabric and leave them for several days. There are drapery sprays available through drapery stores which can be sprayed on fabric to help set the folds while they are bundled.

DRAPES WITH CUSTOM PLEATS©

Custom Pleats© by Decorative Aides, Inc. may be the greatest thing since sliced bread when it comes to using a pleater tape system. Inventor Terry Bressler was struck with the idea one night and worked it out on toilet tissue before perfecting it and making it available to us all. It is, quite simply, a strip of polyester non-woven printed and scored with fold, stitch and tack locations. The resulting drapery has a double fullness ratio, sharp attractive pleats, and uses regular pin hooks--saving the expense and hassle of pleater hooks.

Install rods as described earlier, then measure return + rod + overlap. Figure first pleat at corner of rod then a pleat every 4" along the rod.

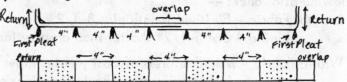

Determining Yardage: Follow steps on pp. 52-55 and use following allowances -
   Length: Finished length + 8-1/2"
      Lining: Cut 5-1/2" shorter than <u>cut</u> drapery length

59

Width: Allow 2x fullness + 4" per panel for side hems and
1/2" for each seam allowance.
Lining: Cut 6" narrower than drapery fabric

1. Follow steps 1 and 2 on p. 56.

2. Turn panel right side out, center lining and press. Stitch top edge with 1/2" seam allowance.

3. Place panel right side up. Dot fabric glue (Wilhold, Quik FabriTrim, Unique Stitch) along seam allowance. Lay Custom Pleats strip onto seam allowance with Tack marks along the top edge. Let glue dry.

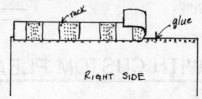

4. Turn and press (use press cloth) tape toward lining side. Glue bottom edge in place (or stitch if desired.)

5. Follow marks on Custom Pleats for folding, stitching, and tacking pleats.

6. See Finishing Touches p. 58.

DRAPES WITH PLEATER TAPE

Determining Yardage: Follow steps on pp. 52-55 and use the following allowances--
  Length: Fabric - Finished length plus 8-1/2"
           Lining - Cut 5-1/2" shorter than drapery fabric

  Width: Fabric - Manufacturers of most pleater tapes use
                  double fullness. Check directions of the
                  brand you purchase
           Lining - Cut 6" narrower than drapery fabric

1. Follow steps one through three on Drapes with Stiffener.

2. Turn the panel inside out like a pillowcase. Center the lining and press with seam allowances toward lining.

3. Baste the top drapery and lining edges together 1/2" from the raw edge. Turn pleater tape ends under 1/2". Lay top edge of pleater tape next to basting stitches on right side of drapery, and stitch in place. Align pockets on tape so pleats fall on corners of rod.

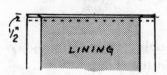

LINING

FOLD UNDER

DRAPERY
(RIGHT SIDE)

4. Turn pleater tape to wrong side of drapery. Press. Stitch bottom edge of tape being careful NOT to stitch pockets closed. Tack or fuse edges of pleater tape.

TACK SIDES

LINING

5. Insert pleater hooks and hang draperies. See finishing touches pp. 58-59...drapery weights and setting pleats.

SHIRRED DRAPES

These are extremely attractive gathered on wooden pole rods. The ruffled heading gives a great decorative touch. Drapes in this style may be left unlined if preferred, but the lining adds body and protection. For a professional look combine drapes with roller shades, Roman shades, or sheers.

Determining Yardage: Follow general measuring information on pp. 52-55, but note that heading on shirred drapes begins 2" above the pole or rod.

Length: Fabric – Finished length plus 13"
Lining – Finished length minus 1"

Width: Fabric – Use 2-1/2X fullness for most fabrics plus
4" per panel for side hems
Lining – Cut 3" narrower than drapery fabric

1. Cut, seam and press panel lengths for drapery and lining fabrics. (Be sure you have allowed for pattern match on drapery fabric.)

2. Turn, press and stitch a 4" double hem in the drapery fabric; and a 2" double hem in the lining fabric.

3. Fold and press a 5" heading on the top of the drapery. Press heading toward the RIGHT side.

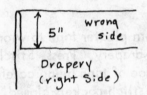

4. Center lining on right side of drapery, matching cut edges. Note that the drapery fabric will extend 1-1/2" on each side of the lining. Pin, then stitch a 1/2" seam. Press the seam allowance up.

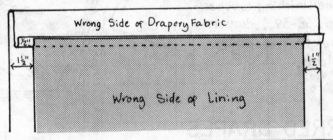

5. Slide side edges of lining over so they are even with the side edges of the drapery. Pin edges in place and stitch 1/2" seams.

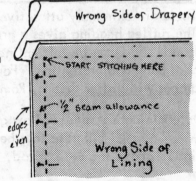

6. Turn drapery right side out. Press, centering the lining so that 1" hems are visible on each side. Stitch across the top of the drapery 4-1/2" from the top folded edge. Stitch again 2" down from top folded edge. Fold the bottom side seams into a miter and hand tack in place.

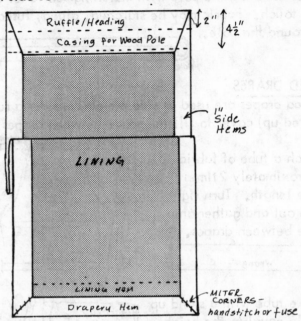

7. Make tie backs by cutting a strip of fabric approximately 7" wide and desired length. (To determine width and length hang drapery in window and pull back with a strip of fabric until desired effect is achieved. Measure length needed and add seam allowances.) Seam long edges. If desired add a strip of iron-on interfacing for body. Turn tie back right side out and press.

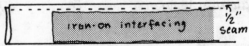

8. Turn raw ends inside and stitch. Fold both ends to a point and tack to plastic or metal curtain rings. Anchor tie backs to hooks fastened to outside of window frame.

FABRIC COVERED WOOD POLES

PLEATED DRAPES

If pleated drapes will hang on wood poles from wooden rings, consider covering the pole with matching fabric for a real custom touch. Fabric may be starched, glued, fused, or stapled around the pole.

pole

SHIRRED DRAPES

If shirred drapes are used as side panels consider a ruched (gathered up) cover to fill the space between drapes.

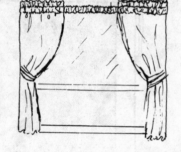

1. Stitch a tube of fabric approximately 2 times pole length. Turn right side out and gather onto pole between drapes. **OR**

   wrong side

2. Make tube with a stand up ruffle equal to the height of the ruffle on drapes and 2 times the length of the space to be filled.

   Stand-up Ruffle →

   Casing for Pole

   Shirred Drape

NOTE: A simple ruched tube of fabric also makes a great addition for the chain of a lamp or planter.

HOURGLASS CURTAIN

The trick to making this curtain so it is taut and smooth in the center with nipped in sides is the addition of length (stretch allowance) at the outside edges. Thus the style lends itself to all-over designs, solids or sheers--fabrics that have definite horizontal motifs would be somewhat distorted in the construction.

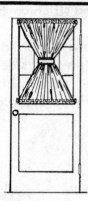

1. Measure finished length. Then add hem allowances (see note):

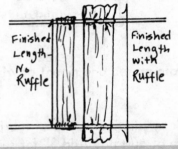

    1. No Ruffle
Finished length plus allowance for top and bottom hems (approx. 4" for double 1" hem.)

    2. With 1" Ruffle
Finished length plus allowance for hems and ruffle (approx. 7 ")

Note: Pin scrap of fabric to rods to help determine correct measurements. Amounts added may need to be adjusted for different ruffle height or size of curtain rod.

2. Measure finished width and add 4" (for double 1" hems).

3. Make a paper pattern of the window or mark the finished dimensions on your work surface. Then plot the stretch allowance of the hourglass with tape measures or string.

Note: The 'waist' of the hourglass should be no less than 1/3 the width of the window.

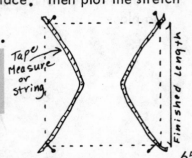

4. Cut and seam panels if needed. Turn, press and stitch double 1" side hems.

5. Fold curtain in half lengthwise. With right sides together, center and mark finished length on fold. Trim away excess fabric.

Trim Away — fold

Finished Length Plus Hem Allowance

Wrong Side

Stretch Allowance Plus Hem Allowance

Trim Away

6. Make rod pockets:

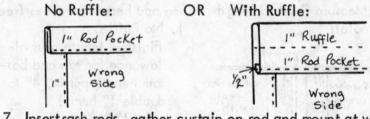

No Ruffle: OR   With Ruffle:

1" Rod Pocket

Wrong Side

1"

1" Ruffle

1" Rod Pocket

½"

Wrong Side

7. Insert sash rods, gather curtain on rod and mount at window. Adjust gathers.

8. Determine length of tieback by pinning a strip of fabric 2" or 3" wide around middle of curtain. Add 3" for seam allowance and overlap. See step 7, p. 63 . Fold in half lengthwise, seam long edges, turn right side out. Tuck ends in 1/2" and fuse (see p. 94) or glue closed.

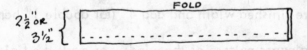

2½" OR 3½" { FOLD

9. Wrap tieback around curtain and slipstitch or pin in place.

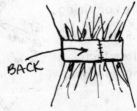

BACK

DOUBLE-SHIRRED DRAPES

Here's a treatment that creates a 'built-in' cornice with none of the fuss or bother. It is also good when you want to add apparent height to a window.

Install two sets of rods at the window--one at the top of the window itself, the other 8" to 12" above.

When measuring for length of your lined or unlined drape, allow for height of 'cornice' plus stand-up ruffle and add 1" for take up on rods.

Stitch casings; one for each rod. Slide drapes onto rods, adjust gathers and enjoy! You may combine them over sheer or casement curtains, shades or shutters.

CARE AND UPKEEP

A new garment or fabric never looks quite as crisp and clean after it has been cleaned or laundered, and it tends to soil faster once the sizings and finishes have been removed. The same is true of drapes and curtains, so the best rule is to put off cleaning or laundering as long as possible, and then do it only as often as necessary. (Sounds great for those of us who hate to clean.) This doesn't mean to ignore your window treatments, however. A couple of steps can help increase their life by two or three times, and reduce the number of times they are subjected to harsher cleaning that can cause shrinking or worse yet, disintegration of sun weakened fibers.

1. Vaccuum draperies often. It really doesn't take long, and the freshness to your room is an added benefit.

(While you're at it, run the dusting attachment over windows and sills to keep window and woodwork cleaning to a minimum as well.) Keeping the dirt from settling in is the first step to extending the life of your drapes and prolonging the inevitable cleaning.

2. If and when additional cleaning is warranted, remove drapes and remove ALL PINS. Then put one panel at a time into the dryer and set controls for the air fluff, NO-HEAT cycle. In addition add a sheet of fabric softener and a 100% cotton terry towel. The towel is to absorb dirt released in the tumbling and the fabric softener is for a fresh clean smell. Let drapes tumble about 30 minutes.

Put drapes up at once to avoid pressing as much as possible, though some pressing or steaming may be needed.

Once drapes have been through the dryer process several times, they may need an actual cleaning or laundering. But at least you have forestalled it as long as possible.

WINDOW IDEAS

The following ideas require a minimum of fabric to create unusual window effects. You may wish to adapt and alter them to fit your own needs.

Kerchief Panels

Two flat panels of fabric sewn to fit the window are suspended from a dowel or cafe curtain rod, and are folded back to create a unique flat window treatment.

Use two contrasting colors or prints for special effects.

Note: Be sure to measure each window separately.

Make each panel half the width of the window plus 1"; and the height of the window plus 3" for hem and seam allowances.

Cut four pieces of fabric (two each from different colors), and stitch 1/2" seam allowances as shown leaving 1 1/2" openings at top.

Fold under 1/2" and then 2" at bottom for hem. Sew hem by hand.

Turn inside out. Press.

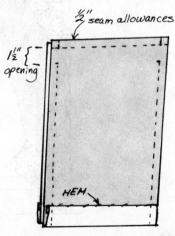

1/2" seam allowances

1 1/2" opening

HEM

69

Sew a row of stitching 1 1/2"
down from top to form casing
for rod.

Sew a plastic curtain ring or
fabric loop 1/2 way down on
inside edges.

Hang curtains in window. Fold
back and attach ring to cup hook
or ornamental hook or knob.

Kerchief panels can be found on long narrow windows as
well as on the shorter type illustrated above. Occasionally
they are placed in a little used doorway.

Other variations feature slightly gathered panels held back in
this manner, and many flat tab ties stitched to the top edge
instead of the casing. The ties are then looped around a
wood pole rod and knotted for a decorative effect.

Try these
simple panel
curtains
on long
narrow
windows
and door-
ways, too.

Another idea uses the panels as shower curtains (Liner goes under or glass door,) for a unique tailored look. They are sometimes installed on a tension rod rather than on the shower rod itself.

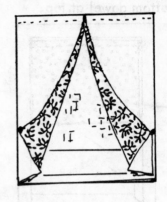

Flat Shade

This treatment consists of a flat panel of fabric with three casings. Dowels are slipped through the casings, and the shade can then be adjusted by re-positioning the dowels as illustrated by the four drawings that follow.

This treatment is flat in appearance, somewhat similar to a roller shade. It is particularly effective for windows where hanging plants are used. Add a cornice for a custom touch. Try it in rentals--for minimum investment.

Shade flat, top dowel in place.

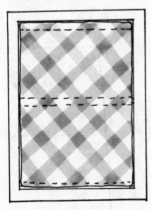

Center dowel in place. (Top folded down.)

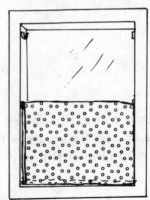

Bottom dowel at top.

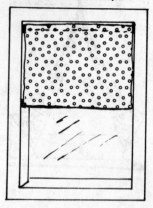

All dowels on top.

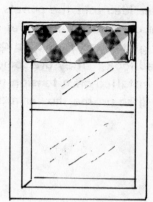

FABRIC PANELS

Install brackets first. Then measure for fabric, adding 1" to width
and length for seam allowances.

Seam right sides together. Leave
1/2" openings as indicated (for
dowels), and an opening in side
for turning the panel.
Trim corners, turn and press
panels.

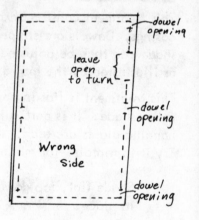

Stitch casings for dowels so
the dowels fit snugly with minimum turning or sliding.

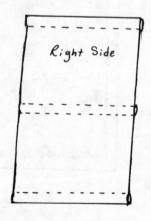

INSIDE MOUNT

For windows with enough depth to
install the pole brackets. Dowels
will be cut to fit inside brackets.
Shade width must be cut to accommodate the brackets.

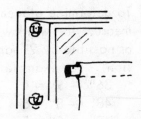

OUTSIDE MOUNT

For windows too shallow for
pole brackets. Screw hooks
are installed at top and center
of window. Screw eyes are
positioned on ends of dowels.

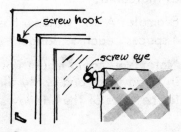

screw hook

screw eye

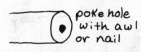 poke hole with awl or nail

Use nail or wire
to help turn screw
eye...or use
screw
hooks →

Note: Top hook must be long enough to accommodate all
three dowels. Center hook holds only two.

Should you prefer, the dowel method that follows could
be adapted for this window treatment as well.

Roman Panels

This is a variation of a Roman
shade. It is moved manually,
however, on a system of dowels.
It is most appropriate for narrower
windows, since it can become
heavy and awkward with too much
width. The advantage is that
either the top or bottom part of
the window may be uncovered,
by re-positioning the fabric panel
and crosswise dowels.

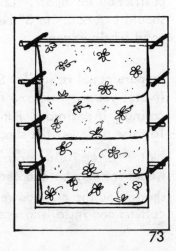

73

To determine placement of dowels and length of panel measure the window opening length. Divide that as evenly as possible by 9" (or 8" or 10"--to obtain nearest even division). For example:

36" ÷ 9" = 4	Use 9" for a 36" window	
48" ÷ 8" = 6	Use 8" for a 48" window	
45" ÷ 9" = 5	Use 9" for a 45" window	

Position dowels by drilling shallow hole at a slight angle, then gluing dowels in place as indicated.

Example: A 36" window has 4 spaces, each 9" long.

Note: You could mount dowels in wood strips and apply them to the sides of the window.

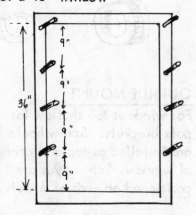

The fabric panel will be twice as long as the window opening, divided into the same number of spaces as created by the dowels. Thus for the 36" window above, the panel would be 2 yds. long--with dowel casings positioned 18" apart. Dowels should extend 2" to 3" beyond fabric edges.

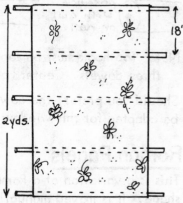

Prepare panel as in Flat Shade Method previously described. (Note: you may use one fabric, with sewn-on strips for casings, if desired.) Panel can now be positioned at window. To raise or lower the shade, re-position the cross dowels.

Note: For an inside mount, this treatment may be adapted by shortening the cross dowels and cutting and installing wood 'rests.'

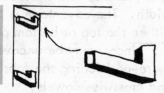

74

Swing Out Panels

Simple swing out panels for summer are made-to-fit frames covered with semi-sheer fabric. Short sticks prop panels open for more ventilation.

Wrapping technique is the same used for folding screens or stretcher bar art.

The same frames could be winterized with heavier fabric or fiber fill in center and lining over back. Weatherstripping increases efficiency.

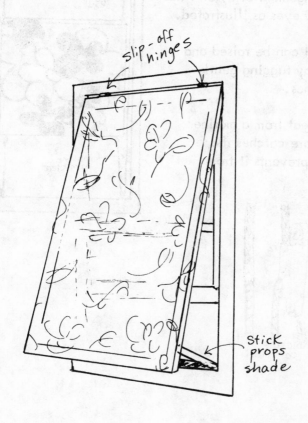

slip-off hinges

Stick props shade

Moveable Panels

Fabric wrapped stretcher bars can be raised and lowered in a window to block view or sunlight.

Wrap fabric around stretcher bars or wood framework. (See p. 99)

Staple back of panel with muslin or drapery lining to help prevent fading.

Suspend the panel on a pulley-like arrangement of nylon lines and screw eyes as illustrated.

The panel can be raised and lowered by tugging gently on the lines.

A cam cleat from a marine supply store catches the line and prevents it from slipping.

nylon rope

screw eye

marine cam cleat

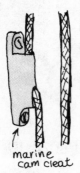

marine cam cleat

PILLOWS

KNIFE EDGE

These pillows are among the simplest to
make, and the most widely used. They
are thicker in the middle and taper to
the edges. The opening through which
you insert filler or pillow liner may be
closed with a zipper or by hand.

1. Cut two pieces of fabric the desired pillow size and shape
   plus 1/2" seam allowance all around. Insert a zipper if
   desired, then stitch all sides.
   Trim corners, turn pillow right
   side out. Press; insert liner or
   stuffing.

   zipper or opening for stuffing

   Note: A pillow liner can be
   made from muslin or a sheet. It
   is actually a separate pillow in-
   serted into the cover, and it makes cleaning and changing
   pillow covers much easier.

   Hint: To keep light weight fabrics sharp in
   the corners you may want to fuse an iron-
   on interfacing to each corner before stitching
   the pillow.

   iron-on interfacing

HAREM

This is my favorite! Elegant and Easy!!

1. Cut two squares or rectangles of
   fabric slightly larger than the desired finished size. (Depth of pillow
   when stuffed will reduce overall dimensions.)
   Make a knife edge pillow as described above. Zipper,
   if used, should be at least 5" shorter than seam, so it
   will not be tied into corners later.

77

2. Mark a light line across each corner on an angle and about 2" to 2-1/2" down from the corner. Gather evenly between your fingers and tie securely with string. Do not cut or trim corners. Turn cover right side out.

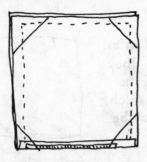 

3. Sew a liner from muslin or a sheet, making it a couple of inches larger than the pillow cover. Do not tie the corners. Stuff the liner with polyester fiber fill. Close liner, insert in Harem cover. Because the liner is larger than the outside cover, the pillow will be fat and plump.

TURKISH

A soft look, but a bit more complicated than the Harem pillow.

1. Measure and cut two fabric pieces as for Harem pillow.

2. Fold and mark each corner of the two pillow pieces in the following manner: Fold corner in half wrong sides together. Measure half the depth of the pillow and mark with chalk or tailor tack. Clip seam allowance to mark it.

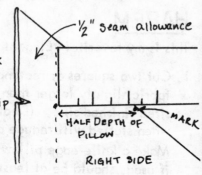

½" seam allowance

CLIP

HALF DEPTH OF PILLOW

MARK

RIGHT SIDE

3. Open the corner out flat, then fold each clip in to the middle. Baste the folds in place. Trim corners.

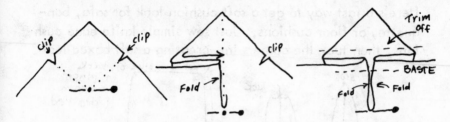

4. Place right sides together and machine baste one seam allowance. Insert zipper. Open zipper, stitch remaining seams and match corners exactly--keeping the folds straight and even. Insert liner or stuff.

TURKISH KNOTTED

Large Turkish cushions can be given an unusual finishing touch with knotted cording. Use the large fat cording (about 1" in diameter), and cover it with a tube of fabric that matches the pillow. For tubing allow for circumference of pillow plus 1-1/2 yd. (Tubing is best cut on the bias, and may be pieced.)

Tack or glue tubing to edge seam of Turkish pillow--tying loose knots so they fall at corners. Start with knot on one corner, continue around pillow and tuck raw end under and into first knot. Tack raw ends.

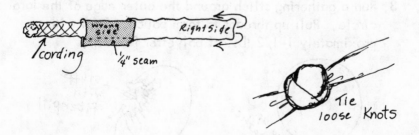
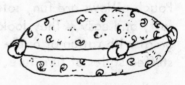

TUCKED CORNERS

Here's a fast way to get a soft cushion look for sofa, ban-
quette, or floor cushions. Just sew simple knife edge cushions, then tuck the corners in--creating a soft boxed look.

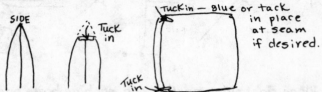

If you want the corners held in place, tack or use glue dot
at seam.

POUCH

Pouch pillows are fun, soft,
fast, and easy. They look
great with rattan or over-
stuffed styles of furniture.

1. From your fabric cut a circle with a 36" diameter. Cut
   one 10" circle from matching fabric and one 10" circle
   for interfacing (matching or contrasting fabric).

2. Stitch the small circles right sides together with a 1/2"
   seam allowance. Stitch entirely around the circle.
   Pull fabrics to separate the layers and carefully cut a
   shash in center of INTERFACING LAYER ONLY. Pull
   fabric through slash, turning circle right side out. Press.

3. Run a gathering stitch around the outer edge of the large
   circle. Pull up threads to form pouch. Stuff with approximately 1-1/2 lbs. of polyester fiberfill.

4. Center the small circle over the opening, slipstitch it in place by hand.

NOTE: For an oblong pouch pillow use a 40" by 32" rectangle of fabric instead of a large circle.

NO-SEW PACKAGE

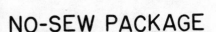

Use a knife edge or box style pillow liner as the base for this easy pillow.

Cut cover fabric 3 times the length of the base pillow.
Place the base pillow diagonally across your fabric.
Fold two opposite sides over pillow, folding raw edge under near center. Fold the remaining two sides toward the middle and tie them in a square knot at center top.

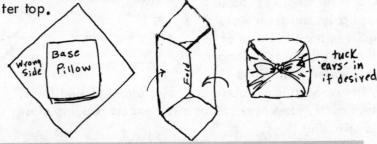

Wrong Side

Base Pillow

Fold

tuck 'ears' in if desired

Note: Use fabric scraps, sheets, or silk scarves to experiment with.

BATH ACCESSORIES

When you make your own toilet accessories you can get away from the fake fur fabrics used in 99% of ready-mades and create a custom touch. Use chintz, gingham, velvet upholstery fabrics, terry cloth, towels, sheets, patchwork, etc. Pad the seat cover with polyester fleece or quilt batting for a soft touch, but it won't be thick, and the lid will stay up!

I love a starch trick I used in our bathroom, where I made fleece lined tank lid and seat covers; but I starched the all cotton chintz directly to the toilet tank. It does get damp from some sweating--but it holds! And it's been there four years. It gets a wash with the sponge when I clean the toilet, and it has never loosened, in which case I would add a little more starch. (See p. 23 & 110 for other starching ideas.) Why not give it a try? You've nothing to lose but a bit of fabric.

TANK LID COVER

1. Cut a rectangle of fabric and polyester fleece or quilt batting the size of the lid plus 2-1/2" longer and wider. Pin fit to lid with wrong side of fabric up. Sew along pinned lines, trim darts, press open. Cut away excess padding close to stitching lines.

   Wrong Side

2. To make casing, open out one folded edge of bias fold tape. Pin tape to lid cover with right sides and raw edges even. Stitch with 1/4" seam.

   folded edge
   open edge
   RIGHT SIDE
   open edge
   folded edge

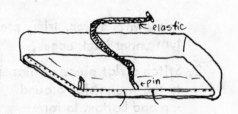

3. Turn bias to inside and press. Stitch folded edge of bias to cover. Leave an opening to insert elastic.

4. Cut a piece of elastic 45" long. Pin safety pin to end for threading, and one large pin across other end crosswise. Pull elastic through casing.

5. Overlap ends of elastic and stitch together securely.

TOILET SEAT COVER

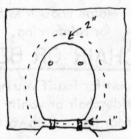

1. Make a pattern by taping a piece of paper to the back of the seat and drawing around it. Add 1-1/2" to 2" around the curved edge, and 1" across the bottom edge.

2. Cut a piece of polyester fleece or quilt batting and a piece of fabric according to the pattern and stitch them together at the outer edge.

3. Make casing by opening out one folded edge of 1/2" single-fold bias tape. With right sides together pin bias to outer edge of cover with raw edges even, curving to fit. (See step 2 above.) Turn tape to wrong side and stitch in place close to the fold.

4. Cut a piece of 1/4" elastic 32" long. Pin safety pin to one end for threading and crosswise on the other end. Thread elastic through casing. Overlap ends of elastic and stitch securely.

TANK COVER

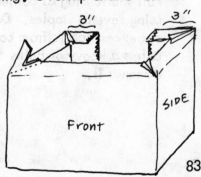

1. Measure around tank ends and front plus 6". Measure height of tank plus 3". Cut fabric and layer of padding. Pin fit darts at top and bottom

as shown. Stitch, trim, press seams open. Zig zag or turn under back edges.

2. Stitch a flat piece of bias to the wrong side around top and bottom to form casing for elastic. Cut two pieces of elastic 36" long. Thread through top and bottom casing as shown. Overlap ends of elastic and stitch securely.

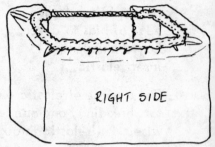

RIGHT SIDE

3. Place cover in position on tank. Make a small slit, just large enough to fit handle through. Zig zag around slit for reinforcing.

CHAIR OR BENCH SEAT

Just for fun if you have enough room in your bath for a side chair or vanity bench, cover the seat to match and coordinate with your room.

1. Measure the depth and width of the seat and add 3" all around. Staple polyester fleece to the seat first for opaquing and padding. Clip to fit as needed. Remove excess bulk from corners with scissors.

2. Wrap and staple fabric in place. Wrap ends first, then sides. Pull fabric snug at corners, using several staples. Do not cut excess fabric from corners unless a heavy or bulky fabric demands it.

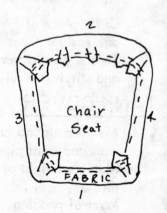

chair seat

Polyester Fleece

Chair Seat

FABRIC

SHOWER CURTAIN

One of the quickest ways to liven up a bath is with the clever use of fabric, and a simple-to-make item like a shower curtain can be a spectacular addition. A standard shower curtain is usually 6' x 6' though you may make it wider or longer to suit your needs.

1. Cut fabric into 81" lengths (or according to your specific dimensions) which allows for double 1" top hem and double 3" bottom hem. Seam the panels together as needed for finished width of 75" or 76".

2. Turn down top edge and make a double 1" hem. Stitch or fuse. Turn up a double 3" hem at the bottom edge; stitch or fuse. Repeat at side edges with a double 1" hem.

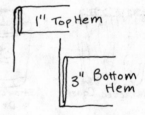

3. Apply grommets, large eyelets, or 5/16" buttonholes along the top edge. Center the plastic liner and use its holes as guides, or space 12 holes evenly along the top of the curtain. Start 1-1/2" from side edges and 1/2" from top.

4. Lay curtain and liner together. Insert shower hooks through both. Mount above tub.

Note: See p. 71 for 'Kerchief' Shower Curtain directions.

ADD A VALANCE

To conceal the shower rod and add height to the treatment, use a spring tension rod and position the valance at the ceiling. Try a ruffled (gathered) flounce or the more tailored

'cornice' look of a flat panel suspended by the top casing.
Either treatment allows air flow for ventilation.

WASTEBASKETS

A simple but effective wastebasket cover can be made following the directions for a gathered lampshade (p. 91). Best of
all, it can be laundered or changed when desired.

I have also enjoyed the effect created by starching on decals
or ribbon strips to a painted basket. Often I just starch a leftover length of coordinating fabric right over the wastebasket,
then trim edges with a razor blade when fabric is dry.

Gathered Cover

Starched Ribbons
& Decals

Starched Fabric
Cover

LAMPSHADES

It is suprisingly easy to cover a lampshade with fabric. You can choose from almost any kind of fabric and from several methods for covering. Whether flared, pleated, or gathered, your new lampshade will prove a bright accent to a room.

Pleated

1. Determine yardage needed.
    A. Height
       For firm fabrics:
       Height of shade + 1/2" = _____ in.
       For fabrics that ravel:
       Height of shade + 1" = _____ in.

    B. Length
       3 x top circumference + 12" = _____ in.

    This formula yields two pleats per inch, each pleat 3/4 inch deep.

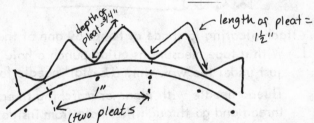

2. To make light fabrics firmer, dip in starch, hang to dry. Press.

3. If fabric is to be pieced, do not seam it. Instead lap one piece on top of the other and fuse. See p. 47.

4. Place strip of non-waxed shelf paper down on large flat surface. Cover with webbing, then fabric. Press till thoroughly bonded. When cool, turn paper side up.

fusible web

fabric

shelf paper

5. Turn 'ravelly' fabric over edge of paper and fuse or glue. OR for firm fabrics trim fabric clean, next to paper.

6. Taking care to KEEP LINES STRAIGHT AND PARALLEL, draw lines 3/4" apart on paper side. Use a see-through plastic rule for ease of marking. Every 8 or 10 pleats, use a carpenter's square or T-square to check that lines are straight.

7. Hold ruler at line and lightly score with blunt object (such as knitting needle). Be careful not to cut through.

8. Fold in accordian pleats. Run flat side of knife or iron over bundle of 5 or 6 pleats to sharpen edges.

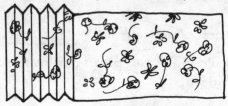

9. Attach pleating to shade or hoops by one of these methods:
   1. With a tape measure as guide punch a hole every 1/2" just under the wire rim. (Use 'fat' needle for punching.)

   Thread needle with clear or matching thread. Anchor thread and go through first hole from inside to outside.

   Barely catch the fold of the pleat. Go back through the same hole and on to the next. Continue around shade.

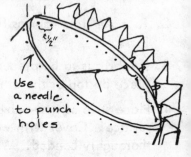

1/2"

Use a needle to punch holes

Bobby pin pleats in place around bottom. Adjust. Put drop of glue under each pleat. Let dry. Remove pins.

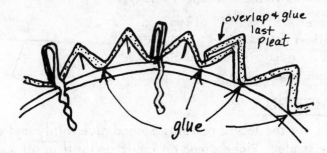

overlap & glue
last
pleat

glue

2. Both top and bottom may be bobby pinned and glued. Divide top of shade equally and make marks for gluing pleats. Glue and pin. Adjust bottom as above.

3. If attaching pleats to wire frame—punch holes 1/4" down from top edge. With yarn loop around top

wire. Repeat for bottom of shade.

10. To finish off, the last pleat should overlap IN and not out. (See sketch at top of page.) Trim off extra pleats. Put glue along last pleat. Clip and let dry. Remove clips.

Flared

MAKING THE SHADE PATTERN

Place the shade on paper. Mark beginning point and roll the shade along, carefully marking top and bottom of shade as you go. Add 1" for overlap.

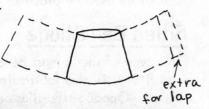

extra
for lap

Note: If you are making a new paper cover for the shade, use your pattern and glue it to the old wire frame. Hold in place with clips or clothespins while glue dries.

Cut out the paper pattern and test it for fit around the shade. Then cut from fabric. Attach to the shade using one of the

89

methods decribed below. Finish off by gluing trim over the raw edges at top and bottom Use a decorator craft glue (such as Wilhold or Super Tacky).

Note: Add on 3/4" at top and bottom if you plan to turn the fabric edges inside and glue them down.

1 extra for overlap

WHITE GLUE

Cut out the fabric pattern. Spread glue thinly and evenly on the shade. Place shade on fabric and roll to attach fabric. Work the fabric with hands to smooth in place. Finish top and bottom edges.

SPRAY ADHESIVE

Cut fabric pattern. Spray fabric evenly with adhesive, such as SpraMent, PhotoMount by 3M. Press fabric onto shade. This works best on smooth surface shades.

STARCH

Smooth surface shades starch very well. Spread starch on shade using a sponge. Smooth fabric pattern into place. Let dry. Finish with trim.

FUSING

Cut fabric pattern and matching piece of fusible web. Place fusible on the shade, fabric on top. Use short strokes, working around the shade, overlapping fabric. Note: Hot iron cannot be used on plastic.

Fitted Bell Shade

This type of shade must be cut on the bias to insure stretch and fit. It is also fabric lined, so four fabric pieces must be cut. Opaque silk-like or taffeta-like fabrics work best.

1. Wrap all ribs and hoops tightly with narrow strips of twill tape or hem tape. This is optional, but gives a more professional finished product.

2. Pin fabric to shade, wrong sides out and on the bias to establish seam lines. Fabric should be pinned so seams

fall on top of ribs. Use clothes pins to hold fabric in place at top and bottom and to prevent marring fabric.

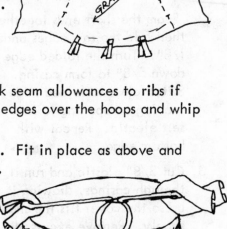

Trim away excess fabric leaving 1" extra at top and bottom. Stitch seams.

Adjust outside shade in place, again using clothes pins to hold fabric to the hoops. Tack seam allowances to ribs if needed. Fold top and bottom edges over the hoops and whip into place.

Position lining inside of shade. Fit in place as above and whip to outside edge of shade. Make small cuts at braces to allow lining to fit smoothly.

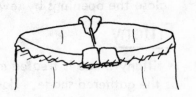

Cut and fold a strip of shade fabric and wrap it around top braces, hiding the small cuts in lining fabric. Tack in place at top outside edges. Trim ends.

Attach trim to cover raw edges at top and bottom Use bias folded strips of the shade fabric, or other trims of your choice.

Note: It is possible (though not necessarily easier) to cut this shade with one seam by rolling shade for pattern and cutting on bias. The fabric is then stretched very taut to complete the shaping and locate the seam.

Gathered

This is a very attractive soft shade. It is simply a gathered casing, which can be slipped over the shade. A definite advantage is that it can be removed, washed, and replaced.

Note: The same technique can be used to make wastebasket covers, flower pot or planter covers, etc.

1. Cut a strip of fabric equal to:
   Height of shade + 4"
   Circumference of shade x 2
   Note: The strip may be
   seamed if necessary. Seams
   can be hidden in gathers.

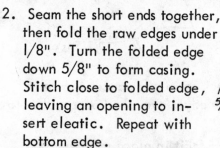 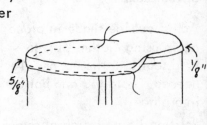

2. Seam the short ends together,
   then fold the raw edges under
   1/8". Turn the folded edge
   down 5/8" to form casing.
   Stitch close to folded edge,
   leaving an opening to insert eleatic. Repeat with
   bottom edge.

3. Cut 3/8" elastic and run it
   through casings, drawing it
   up so the cover fits the shade
   snugly. Remove excess elastic, sew ends together, and
   close the openings by sewing.

Tiffany

A tiffany shade is treated much the same
as the gathered shade. However, since
the top is considerably smaller than the
bottom--the fabric strip is cut the cir-

cumference of the shade plus 2", (double fullness would crea
create much too much fabric at the top), and the height of
the shade plus 4".

Follow directions for sewing the gathered shade.

Another variation can be obtained by
adding 3" more to the height of the
shade to create a standing ruffle at the
top.

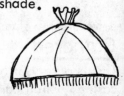

Note: Tiffany frames are available from many fabric stores
and from craft and hobby shops as well.

THE FUSIBLES

Fusibles are mentioned throughout this book, but a separate discussion of them and their uses may be helpful.

Stacy's Stitch Witchery, Pellon Fusible Web, Poly Web, Perky Bond--to name the most common--were introduced to the home sewing industry some years ago. They have simplified and revolutionized many techniques!

Basically, they are monofilaments of extremely heat sensitive fiber arranged in a random pattern. They are available by the yard in most fabric stores or fabric departments. They come in 18" widths and in pre-cut strips.

HINT: It is most economical to cut your own strips! Just 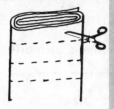 fold the webbing into a roll. Cut through all layers, unfold your newly cut strips!! "Of course, now why didn't I think of that?" I said when a friend showed me this trick. (I had been drawing lines across 'miles' of webbing with pencil and ruler, and then painstakingly cutting each strip.)

HOW DO THEY WORK?
The webbing is placed between two objects, heat is applied, the webbing melts, and the two objects are effectively fused or 'bonded' together.

In decorating fusible webs can be used in two ways--
   1. Fabric to fabric
   2. Fabric to non-fabric

When you add fusibles to your decorating tools, a whole new world will begin to unfold ---

Fabric to Fabric Applications

Always read the directions that come with the webbing!
They will indicate the need to use HEAT, MOISTURE, and
PRESSURE. I would also add PATIENCE.

1. Heat--from an iron
2. Moisture--from an iron PLUS a damp press cloth.
   (The cloth also protects heat sensitive fibers.)
3. PRESSure--NOT a sliding, ironing motion. Use an
   up-down motion. This enables adequate heat to de-
   velop to melt the webbing, and prevents stretching
   the fabric.
4. Time--Your iron must be placed in each position for
   a length of time--up to 10 to 15 seconds--to create
   enough heat for the
   web to melt and BOND
   Completely....
         this takes....

overlapping
iron prints
assure a good bond

5. Patience! But the reward is a beautiful bond with
   no stitches.

TO BOND FABRIC TO FABRIC

A piece of webbing is inserted <u>between</u> two layers of fabric.
For example:
    To fuse a 2" hem:
      Turn up the hem and press.

2" hem

Cut webbing in strip and
insert in hem:
    A. 1 3/4" wide for full-
       bodied hem.

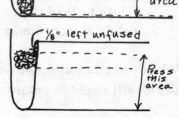

⅛" left unfused

Press this area

    B. 1/2" wide for simple
       hem.

⅛" left unfused

Press this area

To Fuse an Applique Cut From Fabric:

Pin webbing securely to fabric. Cut the two together. Leave pinned. (This prevents shifting of the two pieces.)

Position applique on fabric. Touch iron to a few places to 'baste' the applique. Carefully remove pins.

Lay damp press cloth over applique. Steam and PRESS for 5 to 10 seconds. Allow to cool. Flip fabric and press on wrong side, too. (Resist the urge to peel and peek to see if it is bonded. Let it cool and set.)

Applique edges may be zig-zagged. However, if you cut webbing carefully, keeping it the same size and not allowing it to shift, you may not need any edge finish.

IN CASE YOU'RE WONDERING--

Yes! Fusibles are washable and cleanable WHEN THEY HAVE BEEN PROPERLY APPLIED!

Yes, you will occasionally get some of the fusible on your iron. Easiest ways to clean it off are to use one of the hot iron cleaners (Bottoms Up, Clean and Glide, or Faultless Hot Iron Cleaner), or you will find that rubbing alcohol works on a cool iron.

95

FABRIC TO FABRIC SUGGESTIONS

- Hemming curtains, valances, shower curtains, etc.

- Slip a strip of webbing inside the crease of curtains or draperies to keep the edges from 'billowing' open when curtains are at window.

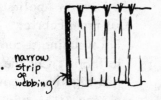

narrow strip of webbing

- Fuse seam allowances down, then turn down casing and stitch in place....

  You can then insert elastic or curtain rods without 'hanging up' under seam allowances.

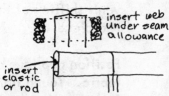

insert web under seam allowance

insert elastic or rod

- Attach appliques, ribbons, trims, bias tape, etc.

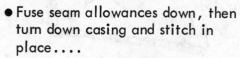

  Note: If you fuse trim first, then stitch it, it will not shift, creep, crawl, or stretch.

- Stiffen and strengthen fabric for cornices.
- Make roller shades. (My book Roller Shades - Make Your Own From Fabric will provide you with a complete reference for making roller shades.)

Fabric to Non-fabric Applications

This is where I really get excited about fusibles, because you can literally bond fabric to cardboard,

wood,

paper,

metal, and

most any non heat-sensitive item.

Do make a test sample or a small project or two. You'll be amazed at how easy it is to cover objects in this way. It is a durable and fairly permanent way to cover with fabric. Soon you'll be covering and creating:

- Picture frames (p. 87)
- Folding screens (p. 46)
- Bookends
- Shelves

96

- Line trunks (plain or patchwork style)
- Line or cover drawer fronts
- Lampshades (pp. 87-92)
- Storage boxes, gift boxes (directions follow)
- Collage wallhangings
- Scrapbook covers
- Etc., etc., etc.

CARDBOARD STORAGE BOX

Use one of the big 'coffee table size' boxes available in notions departments, or small boxes of your choice.

First, measure around the box from each side to determine amount of fabric needed. Position webbing on top of lid, then cover with the fabric. Iron the fabric to the top of the lid.

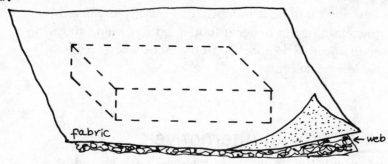

Place the lid upside down on the table and trim away the excess at corners as shown in the diagram.

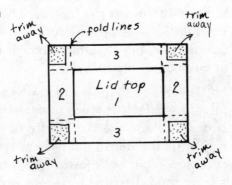

Fuse the sides numbered 2 to the lid, bringing the fabric just around the corner.

Fold sides numbered 3 into place and fuse them to the lid. Add more webbing or a little glue to the fold at corner.

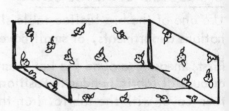

Wrap the fabric to the inside of the lid and fuse.

Treat the bottom of the box in the same manner. Start with the bottom, then two opposite sides, the two ends, and the inside.

The best look and most durability is usually achieved by using webbing solid under a fabric, rather than using strips. However, you will probably find places where strips will do the job adequately.

An Economical Alternative

As an alternative to webbing for some projects, plastic cleaner bags and even plastic wrap (Saran, etc.) can be used as the fusible. Place the layer of plastic between the item to be covered and the fabric. Use as hot an iron as you dare. The plastic serves as the fusible. It usually does not melt completely, but it softens enough to hold the fabric to wood or cardboard in particular.

NOTE: This method should not be used on fabric to fabric application, since it tends to deteriorate with time. However, it is possible to use the plastic as a fusible in a temporary way until the fabric has been stitched down. For example an applique might be 'plastic fused' to position it. Then use zig-zag or hand stitching to secure it permanently. The plastic remains under the applique.

Stretcher Bar Art

Wrap a great fabric find a-
round art stretcher bars (from
art supply or needlework departments). Choose the size
bars you need for each side,
then push the bars together.
Cut fabric at least 2" wider
and longer on each side for
wrapping. Lay the fabric
face down on smooth surface
and center it on your design.

Use push pins to hold it to the bars while you check it from
the front side to be sure everything is straight and centered

Bring fabric up and over the
bars and staple at center top.
Do the same at center bottom,
keeping fabric taut as you work.
Follow the numbered diagram
and keep stapling toward the
corners.

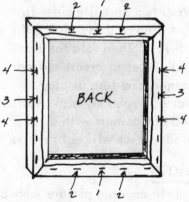

BACK

Finishing the corners is a two-
step process. First smooth the
fabric along the stretcher bar,
then pull it into a mitred fold
and staple it in place.

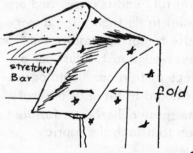

stretcher
Bar

fold

Pick up the remaining fabric and smooth it into a sharp corner, wrap it to the back side and staple it in place on top of the first step.

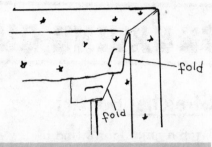

Note: Fabric can also be 'stretched' around a solid piece of wood, cardboard, foam board, cellotex, etc. Depending on the substance you choose, several different techniques may be used to attach the fabric. Consider staples, spray adhesive, starch, fusing.

Frames

To wrap a frame use techniques for mats (which follows) or wrap in this manner using four pieces of fabric each cut about 2" longer then the frame. Wrap two opposite sides first by fusing or spray gluing the fabric. Then fold the two end pieces to create mitred corners and fuse or glue to frame. (You may also overlap and cut corners with a razor blade--bias will not ravel).

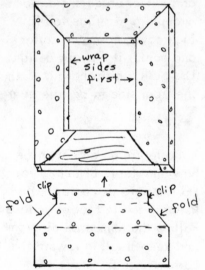

Mats

Fabric covered picture mats are colorful, add texture, and are easier to do than using a mat knife to cut the traditional type bevel-edge mat. Just cut a piece of thin cardboard or poster board to serve as the mat. Use spray adhesive or fusible web to attach the fabric.

100

Clip and trim away fabric in center. Fuse or glue to the back of the mat as illustrated.

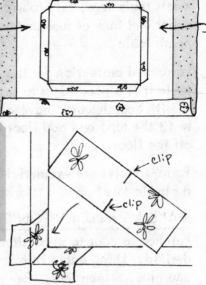

Note: If you use thicker material for mat, frame, or mirror frame--first cover each corner with a small piece of matching fabric--then proceed with the wrapping as described above. (Corrugated cardboard, foam board, plywood, etc. will require this treatment.)

Parsons Table

First, staple, fuse, or glue a layer of polyester fleece (Pellon), Thermolam Plus (Stacy), or needlepunch to the table. Butt cut edges. This pads (fabric clings, noise is reduced), protects--sharp blows won't cut fabric, opaques old color or print, and is well worth the time. Cut fabric 10" longer and wider than table top. Cut leg strips length + 3", and circumference + 3". Start wrapping at inside corner of leg. Clip as needed where leg meets apron. Fold final edge of fabric and glue or fuse in place.

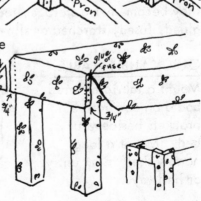

Center top fabric on table. Fold fabric at corner and trim excess (leave 3/4"). Tuck the 3/4" to the inside along corner of table.

Clip top piece where apron
meets table legs, fold fabric
under and tack or fuse underneath table.

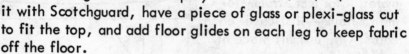

For added protection for the
table it is a good ideas to spray
it with Scotchguard, have a piece of glass or plexi-glass cut
to fit the top, and add floor glides on each leg to keep fabric
off the floor.

Parsons tables are wonderful in all shapes and sizes for adding
a classic touch, and a special look when upholstered.

MAKE A SIMPLE PARSON'S TABLE

Purchase a door to dimensions
desired. Using angle irons
and glue, attach legs. Remember a Parson's table legs
are square, and the same
dimensions as thickness of
the table top.

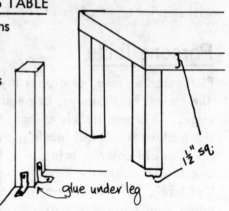

glue under leg

FABRIC COVERED CUBES

Cubes are a simple solution to the end table/coffee table
problem. If cubes are hollow with hinged or lift-off tops
they become extra storage, too. Fabric can be stapled,
glued, fused, starched or slip-covered in place.

QUICK SHELF-TABLE

Mount a fabric covered
board on decorative
brackets beside your
bed. Mount a long
narrow shelf in an entry
or hallway.

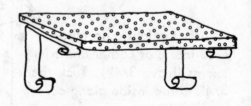

102

Conceal A Shelf

A shelf cover insert can conceal shelf clutter, even stereo speakers. Just make a frame (or use stretcher bars) to fit the shelf opening, with 1/8" clearance all around. Wrap frame with fabric, see p. 99. Add a small pull tab of ribbon for easy removal. Put fabric covered frame in place--friction fit holds it.

Accent A Shelf

Try starching fabric to the wall in the back of your shelves. For the back of a bookcase cut cardboard pieces to fit, then fuse with fabric and push into place. See the magic difference this custom touch gives.

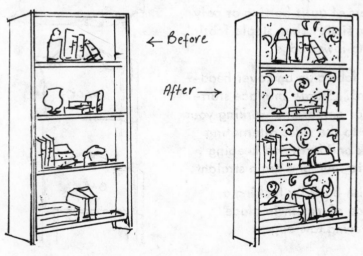

← Before

After →

Bookcases

To cover a bookcase with fabric follow the illustrations to the right.

When covering individual shelves that will sit on bricks or brackets, refer to directions for screens (pp. 49-50).

Consider covering other items--file cabinets, recipe boxes trunks, chairs, etc.

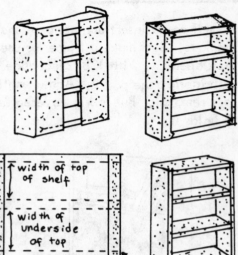

width of top of shelf

width of underside of top

fold (or cut to fit)

Headboards

Use your staple gun and turn a piece of plywood or an old headboard into a new decorator accessory. Cover with layers of quilt batting or poly foam first. Then staple fabric along lower edge.

Pull fabric up and over headboard. Staple in place starting at center and working your way to the sides alternating back and forth and keeping fabric taut and grain straight.

Finish back by tacking a piece of muslin in place covering raw edges.

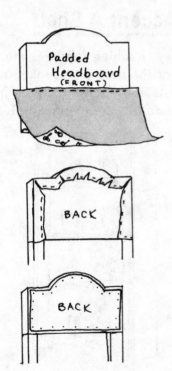

Padded Headboard (FRONT)

BACK

BACK

HANGING HEADBOARD

Make an economical and easy headboard that hangs on the wall. Cut a piece of 1/2" plywood or upson board to desired size. Cut three layers of quilt batting the size of the board plus 2" all around. Cut one layer of fabric (may need to be seamed) the size of the board plus 3" all around.

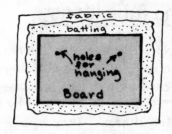

Place batting, then board on top of fabric. Staple batting then fabric snugly to board.

To hang use picture hangars or drill two holes through the board (before wrapping) and hang on two screws anchored to wall studs.

SLIPCOVERED HEADBOARD

Cut two pieces of fabric the size of headboard plus 1/2" seam allowances. Cut strips the width of headboard plus 1/2" seam allowances. Seam together as shown. Press, clip and turn right side out. Slip over headboard and tack in place.

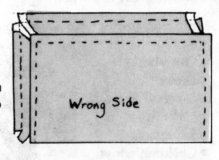

Note: Take measurements AFTER headboard has been padded to assure correct fit of fabric cover.

Patchwork

Boxes, tables, dressers, picture frames, inside of trunks, etc. can be patchworked quickly and permanently by cutting pieces of fabric and fusible web and fusing in place in patchwork design. If desired, seal with Varathane.

Sono Tube Ideas

Sono tubes are concrete forms. They can be located at concrete companies and building construction suppliers. They
are cardboard tubes and come in diameters from 4" to 48".
The tubes are usually sold by the foot--sometimes with a
cutting charge. They have MANY uses for do-it-yourselfers.
One of my favorites is--

PLANT STANDS

Use 8" or 10" sono tubing.
Cut it about 3 feet long or
any length you prefer. Cover
it with fabric or mylar (see
hardware), add a plastic pot
for a liner, then set in your
favorite plant or fern.

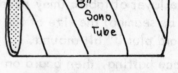

8" Sono Tube

glue or staple fabric
to sono tube

Grouping several planters of
various heights in a corner
creates a great focal point.

Sono tubes of other diameters can form the base for:

- Stools, tables
- Wastebaskets
- Lamps
- Baseball bat racks
- Umbrella stands
- Toy boxes
- Children's toys
- Etc., etc., etc.

Tablecloths

ROUND CLOTHS

1. Measure the table to determine diameter of cloth needed. Decide how much drop you wish-- many prefer round cloths to be floor length.

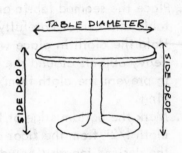

2. Measure from floor to tabletop, across diameter of table and down to the floor on other side. Add 1" extra for hem. Add 1" extra for each seam that will cross through the tablecloth.

3. If fabric is wide enough to accommodate a cloth without seams, fold fabric in quarters. Cut a length of non-stretchy twine to serve as a compass.

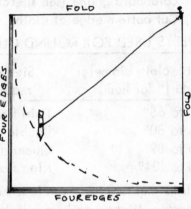

4. Attach the cord to the fabric with a 'corsage' pin through a knot. Tie the twine to a pencil or tailor's chalk.

5. Straight pin fabric layers together to prevent slipping.

6. Mark the outer edge of the cloth with the pencil. Cut, allowing the extra for a hem. Put narrow hem in by hand or by machine.

Note: When a cloth must be seamed to create enough width, it is undesirable to have a seam in the center of the cloth. To avoid this, seam in the following manner. Then follow directions for steps 1 thru 6.

OVAL CLOTHS

Because oval tables very greatly in shape, the bottom hem of an oval cloth should be marked individually according to the shape of the table.

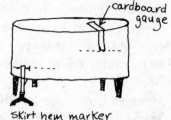
cardboard gauge

1. Place the seamed fabric on the table and center carefully. Hold the cloth in place with heavy objects around the edge to prevent the cloth from slipping.

Skirt hem marker

2. Mark the bottom edge of the cloth 1/2" from the floor or the desired length (including 1" for hem.) Marking of hem may be done with a skirt hem marker, or a folded cardboard gauge (see sketch above).

3. Cut bottom edge of cloth. Hem by machine or hand.

SHEETS USED FOR ROUND CLOTHS

Tablecloth diameter (Add 1" for hem)	Size sheet required	Sheet Dimensions * Width	Length
Up to 65"	Twin flat	66" x	99"
Up to 80"	Double flat	81" x	99"
Up to 89"	Queen flat	90" x	105"
Up to 104"	King flat	108" x	105"

*These measurements exclude hems (for sheets that have a separate stitched on hem.) If the sheet has an attached hem you can remove the stitches and gain about 5" of length.

Napkins

If you are making a new tablecloth, be sure to make some napkins, too. There is a suprising amount of mileage in a yard or two of fabric!

36"x 36"
four napkins

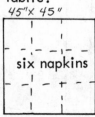
45"x 45"
six napkins

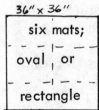
36"x 36"
six mats;
oval or rectangle

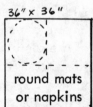
36"x 36"
round mats or napkins

108

Runners

Table runners are versatile additions to your table settings. You may combine them with tablecloths or use them alone. They may be arranged in a number of ways to create interesting table decor.

Make them in a variety of fabrics, lengths and sizes. Length will be

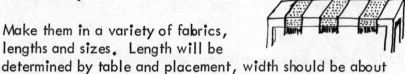

determined by table and placement, width should be about eighteen inches. Remember that reversible runners save time and energy since you gain two sets of runners for a minimum of extra time invested.

Note: Remember the fusibles when it comes to adding appliques or trim to table linens.

WHEN YOU RENT

- Perk up an all-beige apartment. A window swathed in beige takes on new life when trim or fabric border is basted along the hem of the drape. Or add several rows of trim in different colors. When you move, take the trim.

- To liven up a drab window treatment add a lightweight cornice tacked up with straightpins. See p. 57 for cornice ideas.

- Roller shades are decorative and economical. You can use a roller shade that is already there. Take off the old roller and add your own fabric. When you leave staple the old shade back in place. The Shade Book by Judy Lindahl is full of ideas for making your own shades.

- Add your own fabric shower curtain and valance over the one you find in your rental. See section on Bath Accessories for more ideas.

- Make a wall hanging from fabric, towels, scarves, or rugs. Just run dowels through casings top and bottom.

- Frame a pillow case or scarf for instant art.

- Put a plywood round on top of an old table, box, or sono tube. Round cloth hides what's underneath. (This can be an excellent place for hidden storage, too.

Drape boxes or tables, too. More storage!

- Create decals by cutting flowers or other objects from fabric. Dip in starch and apply to doors, walls, valances, soffits, etc. Just smooth into place, sponge off excess starch. Let dry. To remove just dampen and peel off.

- Create borders on window frames, around doors, along ceiling, etc. by dipping satin ribbon in starch and then apply as above.

- For quick cafe curtains open out a pair of pillow cases. Press under 1/4" along side edges. Then turn press and stitch 1" side hems.

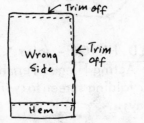 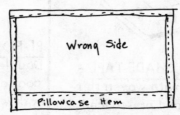

Turn down 1/2" along top edge. Turn, press and stitch 1" hem. Use clip-on cafe rings or insert rod through top hem.

- Use colorful bandanas draped over curtain rod for quick valance treatment.

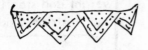

HARDWARE / NOTIONS

ANGLE IRON - An L-shaped bar of metal used for joining two pieces of wood or metal. For example: joining cornice to wall, mounting board to window frame.

AUSTRIAN SHADE TAPE - Twill tape with woven shirring cords and pre-spaced plastic rings. Used to make Austrian shades.

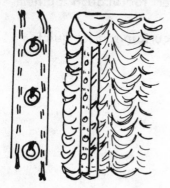

AWL - A sharp pointed tool used for starting holes before screw or nail is inserted.

AWNING CLEAT - Small device attached to side of window frame. Used to secure cords for Roman, Austrian, or bamboo shades.

BI-FOLD HINGE - (also Double Acting Hinge.) Permit door or folding screen to swing both ways.

BRASS WEIGHT ROD - Solid metal rod used for added weight and stability for Roman and Austrian shades.

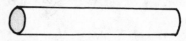

BUTT JOINT - A joint made by fastening two pieces of wood end to end, edge to edge, or end to edge.

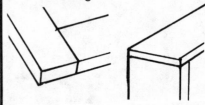

CURRUGATED FASTENER –

(or wiggle-tail). Small grooved metal strip. Used to form joints, as in screens and window frames, or to tighten loose joints

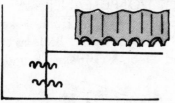

FOAM BOARD – Smooth tagboard with layer of lightweight foam in the middle. Strong and light. Easily cut into shapes. Available at display, art supply, or lumber stores in 1/4", 1/2", and sometimes 1".

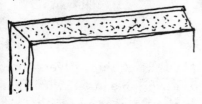

FURRING STRIPS – Thin wood strips attached to wall when the surface is rough or uneven. Fabric or paneling is then attached to furring stirps. Lumber supply.

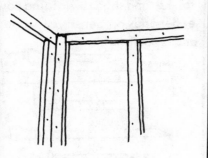

FUSIBLE WEBS – (Stitch Witchery, Pellon Fusible Web). Meltable webs of synthetic fibers. Placed between objects, heated with iron, they melt & fuse the materials together.

HOLLOW WALL FASTENERS –

Special screws used when necessary to drive into wall where there are no studs. Here are three examples.

Plastic Expansion Anchors – For medium weight articles like small shelves, drapery hardware, soap dishes. Plastic sleeve is tapped into hole in wall. As the screw goes in the sleeve spreads to grip the wall. Get size long enough to pass thru wall. If the sleeve is too short, it won't work.

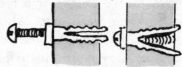

Molly Screw Anchor – Stronger then above method. Slips thru hole and fans out and up to grip wall as it's screwed in. Molly is set if screw begins to turn hard, and if flange under screw head begins to turn with the screw.

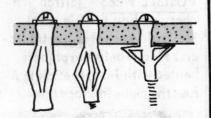

Toggle Bolts - Strongest of all. Used for really heavy things or use smaller size when other types won't hold. Wings open out after they are pushed thru the hole, and open and spread as bolt is tightened.

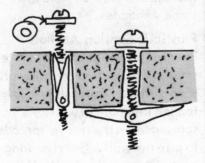

HOMOSOTE - Fiber or composition board similar to cellotex, but firmer. Light, inexpensive, easy to use. Ideal for cornices and covered panels.

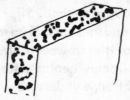

HOOK AND EYE TAPE -
Use for cornices, dust ruffles. Available by the yard.

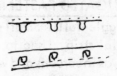

HOT IRON CLEANER - A fabric store notion item. Takes off fusible residue. Bottoms Up, and Clean & Glide are brands.

LIQUID STARCH - Used undiluted to apply fabric to walls and other surfaces.

MYLAR - A shiny silver or gold film available in 54" wide from display stores or art supply. Use for mirror or chrome look.

NAILS - Are classed according to size and shape. Holding power depends on density of wood and type of nail.

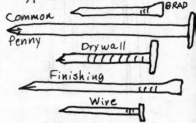

Brads – Small, fine nails used in attaching molding, and all fine work.

Common – General purpose. Used in construction and for rough work. Large head.

Drywall – Large head. Tiny grooves on shaft make them difficult to pull out. For sheetrock.

Finishing – Used on trim and cabinetwork head needs to be concealed. Head is sunk then filled over.

Wire – Fine nail with flat head.

PLUMB BOB – A weight attached to the end of a line. Line is rubbed with chalk and then snapped against the wall to mark true vertical.

POLYESTER FLEECE – Washable, cleanable, 1/8" thick polyester. Use for padding and opaqueing. In fabric stores.

PUSH PINS – Useful for holding fabric in place on cornices, walls, stretcher bars.

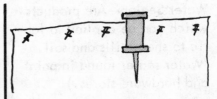

ROMAN SHADE TAPE – Has plastic rings sewn to tape at intervals. Sew tape to fabric, run cord up thru rings causing shade to pleat itself as it is drawn.

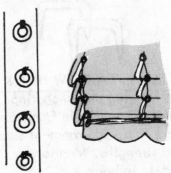

SKOTCH WOOD JOINER – Same uses as corrugated fasteners. These sharp toothed clips hold two pieces of wood securely, and are easy to pound into the wood.

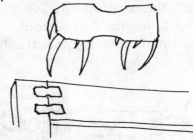

SCOTCHGUARD – ZePel, Amway Dri Guard, Thompson

Water Sealer--Are products which can be applied to fabric to shed spills and soil. (Water sealer found in paint and hardware stores.)

SCREEN STAPLE - May be used in cornice techniques. From hardware store.

SCREW EYE/SCREW HOOK - For hanging and anchoring objects. Available from hardware in a wide range of sizes and strengths. Mentioned widely in book.

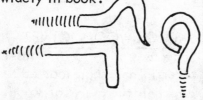

SHIRRING TAPE - A woven tape with heavier cords woven into the construction. Sew flat to fabric. Pull up cords and fabric gathers automatically.

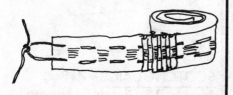

SNAP TAPE - Fabric tape with snaps attached at regular intervals. Can be sewn, or tacked or glued to wood.

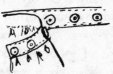

SONO TUBE - Cardboard concrete form. Available from concrete company or building construction supply.

SPRAY GLUE - Aerosol adhesives are found in art supply stores. SpraMent by 3M is a common brand.

SQUARE - Metal L-shaped ruler, used to determine if edges are 'true', and for perfect 90° angles. Use with stretcher bars, roller shades and other projects.

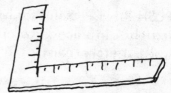

STAPLE GUN – Device which shoots staples with force. Used extensively to apply fabric to wall, screens, etc.

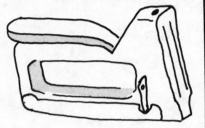

STRAIGHT PINS – When driven into a plasterboard wall until just a bit is exposed, it is suprisingly strong. Hang pictures, fabrics, trims with pins. Nearly invisible mark is left when it is removed.

TOENAILING – Driving nails at an angle in order to fasten one piece of wood to the side of another.

UPHOLSTERER'S TAPE – Narrow cardboard tape available in strips or rolls from upholstery supply. Used for sharp hidden edges and seams.

UPSON BOARD – Cardboard composition board. Can be sawed easily into shapes. Use for cornices and other wall treatments. From lumber supply in 1/4", 3/16", & 1/2".

VELCRO – Nylon fastener tape with hooks on one side, fuzzy surface on the other. Can be sewn, tacked, or fused. Many used in decorating. From fabric stores.

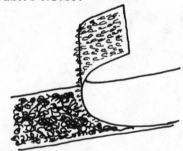

WHITE GLUE – All-purpose glues like Sobo have many general uses. Decorator craft glues (Wilhold, Fab Trim, Mighty Tacky) dry faster, stay flexible, and don't soak thru fabric. Use for trims on lampshades, roller shades, etc.

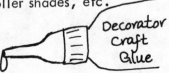

Decorator Craft Glue

NOTES

NOTES

NOTES

METRIC EQUIVALENCY CHART

This chart gives the standard equivalents as approved by the Pattern Fashion Industry.

Converting Inches into Millimeters and Centimeters.
(Slightly rounded for your convenience.)

mm = millimeters   cm = centimeters   m = meters

inches	mm/cm
⅛	3mm
¼	6mm
⅜	1cm
½	1,3cm
⅝	1,5cm
¾	2cm
⅞	2,2cm
1	2,5cm
1¼	3,2cm
1½	3,8cm
1¾	4,5cm
2	5cm
2½	6,5cm
3	7,5cm
3½	9cm
4	10cm
4½	11,5cm
5	12,5cm
5½	14cm
6	15cm
7	18
8	20,5
9	23
10	25,5
11	28
12	30,5
13	33
14	35,5
15	38
16	40,5
17	43

inches	cm
18	46
19	48,5
20	51
21	53,5
22	56
23	85,5
24	61
25	63,5
26	66
27	68,5
28	71
29	73,5
30	76
31	79
32	81,5
33	84
34	86,5
35	89
36	91,5
37	94
38	96,5
39	99
40	101,5
41	104
42	106,5
43	109
44	112
45	114,5
46	117
47	119,5
48	122
49	124,5
50	127

OTHER BOOKS BY JUDY LINDAHL

ENERGY SAVING DECORATING

Easy to read and understand ideas
and instructions for creating a more
energy efficient home. Includes
psychological decorating, retrofit-
ting ideas, how-to instructions for
insulating window treatments and
Roman shades, resources, and much
more. Don't miss this great book.
© 1981   128 pp. $6.95

THE SHADE BOOK

How to make your own roller, Roman,
balloon, and Austrian shades. Five
methods of roller shade construction.
Easy to follow directions, time-savers,
notions and hardware information.
Energy tips. Lavishly illustrated with
line drawings and photographs. Choose
from dozens of ideas for hem and cornice accents.
Revised © 1980   128 pp. $6.95

If you are unable to locate these books locally, write for
ordering information to Judy Lindahl, 3211 NE Siskiyou,
Portland, OR 97212, USA or enclose $6.95 per title plus
$1.00 postage and handling. Canadian orders in US Funds.